TEDDY BEAR ART

How To Design and Make Great Teddy Bears
by Jennifer Laing

All photographs are
by Phillip Castleton, of
Sydney Australia

Published by

Hobby
House
Press

Hobby House Press, Inc.
Grantsville, Maryland 21536

DEDICATION

To all the wonderful friends I have made in the bear world, whose friendship (and bears!) I treasure.
This is especially dedicated to the memory of a dear friend and great beart artist Billee Henderson.

ABOUT THE AUTHOR

Always a closet bear-lover, *Jennifer Laing* still has her childhood Steiff and Hermann bears. Her personal collection is small but cherished, a few old Steiff bears and some examples from her favorite international bear artists.

After gaining a B.A. in Science and studying art for two years, Jennifer was a freelance commercial artist and then held a variety of other jobs including aerobics instructor, personal trainer and ski instructor! In 1990 she managed Australia's largest teddy bear shop where she first began making bears; sewing standing up behind the counter in quiet moments.

Jennifer was the first Australian bear artist to work solely in mohair. She hand-stitches all her bears and works alone, only making 70-100 bears a year. She has won many international awards, and is Australia's best known bear artist. Jennifer is active in charity fund-raising, using her bears to help raise money for animal and wildlife conservation groups, such as Libearty and The Sea Shepherd Society.

Jennifer's designs are constantly changing and she generally only makes editions of five or ten. The largest editions she has done are of 25, and they have been for the Walt Disney World Doll and Teddy Bear Conventions (1994, 1995, and 1997). She was also invited back to Disney World for 1996 and 1998, but had to decline due to the size of her waiting list. She cannot take wholesale orders as she has over three years of personal orders on her waiting list.

Jennifer teaches all levels of bear making and her workshops are keenly attended around the world. She is currently working on her fourth bear book.

Front Cover: A bear cub, a dressed cavalier bear, and a four-legged bear. See page 7 for more information.
Back Cover: The author's hand-stitched bears. See page 13 for more information.
Title Page: The little cavalier riding the four-legged bear. Seepage 8 for more information.

Additional copies of this book may be purchased at $17.95 (plus postage and handling) from
Hobby House Press, Inc.
1 Corporate Drive
Grantsville, Maryland 21536
1-800-554-1447
or from your favorite bookstore or dealer.

ISBN: 0-87588-517-9

TABLE OF CONTENTS

FOREWORD

I have been fortunate to experience many careers so far in my (not that long!) life, but I have to admit that making teddy bears for a living has been by far the most satisfying and creative vocation. There seems to be something about our human condition that gives us an urge to create, even if it is in something as seemingly mundane as cooking a nice meal, growing a garden, arranging some flowers, or decorating a Christmas tree. There is great satisfaction to be gained in even the smallest creative acts we perform in our lives. Those people who say they don't possess an artistic bone their bodies still admit that this is so. Perhaps it is something to do with searching for joy and beauty in life, especially in times when those commodities seem hard to find.

Teddy bears are little miracles because they seem to personify both beauty and joy, but more than that they are a real symbol of love. Many people who may not have known about teddy bears' special charms have discovered them when they made their first bear. The world of teddy bear lovers and teddy bear makers is a very pleasant one. Some of my best friends have been made through our shared love of bears.

My first bears were made not that long ago, in early 1990, so my career as a bear artist is not nearly as long and respected as some. Even so, in Australia at that time bear making as a handmade art/craft form was in its infancy. My desire to make well made, traditionally styled bears in the best mohair fabrics kept me going when supplies did not. Mohair, pure wool felt, boot buttons, excelsior and joint systems were all unavailable in this country, as were patterns, kits and classes on the topic. It took a lot of work to track down the materials I needed, from sources literally all over the world, and a lot of problem-solving with design and construction before I could really get going.

The first bear artists in the USA in the early 1970s experienced the same frustrations, as the English bear artists must have done in their turn. We are fortunate now that in many countries around the world there are good bear making supplies available. You will not usually find these at any local fabric shop, as mohair is an expensive and specialized fabric, but there are many national and international mail-order businesses catering solely for the teddy bear maker (see Supply Index.) Supplies can be ordered by catalogue using sample swatches, or suppliers can often be found at teddy bear shows with a good range of their fabrics and accessories. Lately, some specialist teddy bear shops and some craft shops have started stocking mohair, and there are now also many books, patterns and practical classes available on making bears.

All of this means that it is now much easier to get started in bear making, but because of the increasing numbers of people who want to sell their bears it also means that there is a lot more competition out there. Competition is always healthy, as it moves the industry along, not only with fresh ideas but with improved craftsmanship. It also weeds out the mediocre, keeps the quality high and the prices fair.

It is an interesting phenomenon that in spite of the fact that the world's top bear artists are in competition with each other, they are often each other's best friends and freely share bear making tips and new techniques. Small groups of bear artist friends will get together and have "challenges" to make new and different designs, to have fun and push themselves creatively, maybe solve a specific problem, or create something special for each other. Artists who admire each other's work often arrange a swap and each makes a unique bear for the other. There is very little jealousy and a lot of generosity going around, and it has a much more supportive environment than many other businesses. The Internet is certainly helping to spread the camaraderie and the information network that is at the heart of the bear maker's world.

It is not only the other bear makers who make this career such a pleasurable one. Many bear artists (myself included) started off as bear collectors and continue to be so. Because of this we tend to have an excellent client relationship as we can see the market from both sides. Some of our customers also become firm friends and many stay in touch over the years. I don't know of any other business where one receives lovely Christmas and birthday cards from the customers! Teddy bear making is a really special business, whichever side you look at it from.

INTRODUCTION

People find themselves making teddy bears for many different reasons. It may be that they want to make a special bear for a new child in the family, or that they want to re-create that long-lost teddy of their own childhood. Some have tried their hand at making bears after being teddy bear collectors for many years, while others just want to turn their creativity to unexplored areas and discover bears almost by accident. Whatever the reason, love of teddy bears is usually at the core of it. Anyone who has made a bear can tell you of the immense pleasure and satisfaction of being caught up in the magic of seemingly giving life to a unique little creature. This experience has opened up a whole new world and a new way of life for many people. Very few can stop at making just one bear, and this gentle addiction now spreads a bit more love and joy through the world every day.

Teddy bears are so much more than a toy, they are the receptacle of love, dreams and secrets for many a child and many an adult around the world. Those little furry bodies have always meant so much to us as symbols of security and trust. It is not surprising then, that in recent years teddy bears have become highly prized collectors' items, with antique bears fetching ever higher prices and even modern limited edition bears having sound investment value.

Since the early 1970s the teddy bear has evolved a little further, this time through the hands of individual artists creating their own versions of the ideal bear. Made for the adult collector rather than as a child's toy, these bears are known as "artist bears" made by "teddy bear artists", a term coined by Carol-Lynn Rössel-Waugh, one of the first American bear artists. As

Old Bear and Little Woody. A watercolor painting by the author of a much-loved old Steiff bear named "Old Bear" with one of the author's early bears called "Woody." Little Woody has appeared on his own Australia Post 45-cent postage stamp in a 1997 series called Dolls and Bears. Old Bear's owner was very young when she met President Roosevelt in California in 1904 and presented him with a bouquet of flowers. Old Bear still has the President's thank you note!

Carol-Lynn says "The best designers are daring, whimsical outrageous, playing with new concepts, new fabrics; yet their personal style, their way of expressing the 'teddy bear essence', shines through all of these experiments. The past may inspire them, but they use it in unexpected, offbeat ways, not reproducing or copying bears designed by others. Usually, they do limited editions or one-of-a-kind designs." Unique expressions of creativity, artist bears can be masterpieces of design and craftsmanship, and are of course as highly collectable as they are adorable. These sort of teddy bears are now fast approaching an art form and in fact some art galleries can now be found exhibiting one-of-a-kind artist bears.

Anyone who makes a bear will not necessarily be a bear artist creating an artist bear, just as painting a picture does not make you Picasso, but that in no way diminishes the satisfaction to be derived from creating a teddy bear. For those who are truly creative, however, one of the most exciting things about teddy bears today is that it is one of the few craft areas that have a viable commercial application. Not only is it a wonderful way to find creative satisfaction, but if you are fortunate and your work has that special spark it can also be a great vocation.

There are many different ways of making a career out of creating teddy bears, from an individual scale to a truly international one. You can work by yourself from home and make hand-made bears, or artist originals. You can have a cottage industry and hire seamstresses and stuffers to assist you with your designs, and perhaps you might finish off each bear yourself. You may expand to have your own manufacturing business where your designs are made by others in your employ, or you might even work as a designer for another large international bear manufacturer. Talent, skill and imagination will always find its reward, particularly if you add a dash of perseverance.

If you have tried making bears and have caught "the bug", you might be thinking of selling some of your work. It is important to perfect your craftsmanship, which will only come with time and confidence. The main thing that will send you down your newly chosen path to success is your own unique look and style, and that is something that can only be achieved through the development of your own designs and patterns.

There are many how-to books to start you off making bears, and a lot of good patterns and kits now available for you to experiment with. These should all however, be seen as your starting point, and if you plan to sell your work it is important that it be just that; all your own work. Selling bears made from commercial patterns is not only unfair to yourself and the original designer, it could also be an infringement of copyright. More than that though, you are denying yourself the full thrill of making teddy bears.

The most exciting thing about making your own bears comes when they are truly yours, from the original concept or picture in your mind to the finished furry creature in front of you. Such an artistic and creative act can also be the most addictive thing. The difference between making your own bears from your own designs or making up other peoples' patterns is like learning to paint your dreams and emotions or playing it safe and painting by numbers.

When you start designing patterns on your own your ideas will constantly lead you on, often to exciting and unexpected places. You might be surprised to find that your initial mental images of your ideal bear will not remain constant but will evolve over time. As your practical expertise increases you will find that your bears! Proportions may change as your taste changes and your artistic "eye" becomes more refined. Like the donkey with the carrot on a stick in front of it, your ideal bear will stay out of reach because your next bear will always be a better bear. You are only limited by your imagination, and if you have the imagination and vision you can take your creativity anywhere you want it to go.

This is a book for those of you who have tried the commercial patterns, have caught the bear making "bug" and are now wanting to take that next step - the most exciting one of all. Designing and creating your own teddy bears can bring magic into your life!

1. A bear cub, a dressed cavalier bear, and a four-legged bear.

2. The three different bears whose patterns appear in this book: a bear cub, a dressed cavalier bear, and a four-legged bear.

3. The little cavalier riding the four-legged bear, patterns one and three in this book.

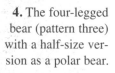**4.** The four-legged bear (pattern three) with a half-size version as a polar bear.

5. The bear cub (pattern two) with another version made to the same pattern by a different Australian artist, Rhonda Harland of Booalbyn Bears.

6. Two lovely 16" (40cm) bears by Australian artist Karla Mahanna, in "antiqued" Alfonzo red and Elliott blue mohair.

7. A wonderful array of miniature bears, all 3" (7.5cm) and under. From left to right: Deb Canham's *Golli*, Rieko Hoshino's *Patches*, Pamm Bacon's red *Belly Button Bear #1*, Octavia Chin's truly tiny *Pooh*, Carolyn Willis' *Bertram and his Golli*, Mac Pohlen's ruffed bear with Reiko Hoshino's tiny penguin, and Evelyn Penfield's *Raggedy Ann*.

8. Some small and special bears by Australian artists. *From left to right:* Loris Hancock's *Blinky and friend* [4-1/2" (11cm) and 2-1/4" (6cm)], Marianne Wagner's *Little Henry* (6" [15cm], made in a limited edition of ten, and modeled after Henry, a large 1908 Steiff in the author's collection), and Rae Hargrave's 1997 TOBY® nominee *Nanouk and coy* (5-1/4" [13cm] and 4-1/2" [11.5cm]).

9. Little *Orlando* in his red vest by Bonnie Windell admires Reiko Hoshino's polar bear, and is joined by Elaine Fujita-Gamble's bear in a romper suit and Ginger Brame's bear in a sweater. All bears are 6" (15cm) or under.

10. Bears aren't the only thing that can be created from mohair! Shown here are Bonnie Windell's opossum, Keiko Toshikura's Papillon dog, a pig jointly made by Bonnie Windell and the author, and a wonderful rat also made by Bonnie.

11. A lovely range of American artist bears, from 6" (15cm) to 14" (35cm). From left to right: Mac Pohlen, Jeanette Warner, Mary George, Mary Ann Wills, Bonnie Windell, and Barbara Conley.

12. A family of beloved old Steiff bears, ranging from 1904 to 1908 and 10" (25cm) to 22" (55cm). From left to right are Bear and Henry, with Sammy and little Buster in front.

13. A selection of old mohair animals from 1900 to 1950, showing a pre-teddy bear era Steiff bear on wheels ridden by a Schuco chimpanzee, a Schuco mechanical "pecking" bird, a Steiff mouse, and American opossum, and a Bing mechanical monkey.

14. Some examples of the author's hand-stitched bears, ranging from 6" (15cm) to 21" (22.5cm). She only makes around 100 bears a year, and all are made to order.

Bear Design

There are many commercial teddy bear patterns and kits readily available today and they come in a wide range of styles from big bears right down to miniatures. Not only are there bears but also bunnies, monkeys, kittens and other animals. These patterns are a good way to experiment with different looks and proportions, as well as to familiarize yourself with the variety of pattern pieces that can go into making a bear. You will find patterns with two-piece bodies and four-piece bodies, one-piece limbs or two-piece limbs, and any number of head pieces from three to six or more. Some bears have tails, some have sewn-in ears, there are many different ways of jointing a bear or fixing in the eyes. Remember the old saying, "There is more than one way to skin a cat"? Well there is definitely more than one way to make a bear!

Making up such diverse designs will give you a good idea of what works for you and what doesn't. That really is the basis for developing your own style, it is a personal feel for the craft. There are also many classes and practical workshops available these days for anyone interested in trying bear making. Some offer different levels of instruction, from the beginner right up to the design process. Even in a beginners class it is fascinating to see that although all the students may be making the same pattern and essentially the same bear, each person will put their individual stamp on their bear's character and no two bears will turn out the same.

Attending workshops is a good way of picking up useful tips and furthering your practical skills. Even if there is only one good tip to be gleaned from a class it is worthwhile, as it all adds to your store of knowledge. Workshops given by well-known bear artists are always in demand, as some have developed their own unique construction techniques. Generous teachers win always share everything they know, and good teachers will always be able to answer even your trickiest question, as well as impart some of their magic to you.

If you have tried a bought pattern you may have found that not all commercial patterns are necessarily good patterns, and some can be more frustrating than satisfying. There have been commercial kits (pre-marked) that have two right arms instead of a pair, and it is not uncommon to find that the head gusset is not long enough to reach the back of the neck! These flaws are somehow always discovered after having cut out your expensive fabric. Often just a little thing, such as lack of definition in the muzzle of the head gusset can lead to irregular pinning and ultimately a skewed muzzle or head.

Such frustrations are often enough to push many people into mak-ing their own patterns. The desire to make a better bear and a more personal bear can often start with adapting a commercial pattern. Perhaps the muzzle was not long enough to suit you, or the feet not the right shape. Already you have started to take creative control and it is not a very big jump to completely creating your own designs. What appeals to you is what designing your own bear is all about.

What makes sense to you may not seem logical to others, but that is not important (unless you are trying to teach a subject, when it is important to be able to get your meaning across). When making your own bears, find what works for you, not only with the appearance of what you are creating but also the techniques you use and the order in which you construct your bear. Everyone does things differently and even a couple of bears which look somewhat similar may have been made using quite different methods.

Patterns can also be designed in several different ways. The starting point is to have a concept or an idea which you want to translate into a three-dimensional work. In other words you can see it in your mind. It may be something which has not been done before and therefore there are no pictures or reference points to work from or it may be an amalgam of ideas you may have seen elsewhere but you want to re-work them in your own style. In either case, it is necessary to "flesh out" your ideas in order to be able to design the right pattern so that your ideas become reality.

If you find drawing easy you may be able to sketch down your ideas free-hand. These preliminary drawings can be a good way of strengthening your concepts. Many people are apprehensive about drawing and are sure that they are not at all artistic, but you don't have to be able to draw or paint a picture to be able to design and make great teddy bears.

If free-hand drawing is not your thing, try some sketches using a simple scale for proportions. This will help make it easier to keep all the parts of the bear coordinated and balanced. This is a good way of giving yourself confidence with your drawing. It is a method often used in life drawing classes when drawing the human form, although people and bears do have somewhat different proportions.

A third way of making a start in your design process may take longer and be messier, but it can also be very accurate. Modeling your bear, either in the finished size or half size, in Plasticine or modeling clay is a great way of creating your ideas in 3D before you actually make the pattern. Some top manufacturers of teddy bears and other toy animals have used this technique over the years, as have many car design companies. Sculpting your bear enables you to make many small or large changes before your begin your pattern process; but better still you can even get your pattern directly from the sculpted form

Modeling System

Starting with a quantity of modeling clay or Plasticine, find an old board to use as a base. If your figure is going to be quite large, you might like to roughly nail in a short upright length of dowel and scrunch a small piece of chicken wire around it. This will act as a support and strengthen your form It also means that you will not have to use so much clay in building up the shape before you start modeling.

You may choose to have your figure standing or seated, but often a seated one is easier to shape while a standing figure may give you a better feeling for the proportions. Continuously turn the board or move around it as you sculpt in order to give you a proper three-dimensional aspect. Some sculptors use a pottery wheel which they can turn by hand.

Once you are happy with the overall look, concentrate on the details and mark in the eyes, nose and paw pads. When the model is finished you can then use it to make up a precise pattern. Using your knowledge of bear making from the different patterns you have already worked with, mark lines on the bear with a pointed tool which will correspond with his seams. If he has an unusual head shape, for example, work out how that shape may best be achieved and mark his seams accordingly.

After drawing on all the seam lines you will need, take some scrap material or even paper towel and pin it directly on to the model. The pins can go straight in to hold the pieces in place. Cut away accurately to match up with the seam lines and when you have done each piece you will have your complete pattern (less the seam allowances.) The ears you may need to remove and flatten out in order to accurately gauge their shape and size. If your figure is seated you may have to use a "guesstimate" to deduce the final length of the body as you cannot pin under the legs.

If your model is smaller than the finished size you intend your bear to be, trace the pattern pieces on sheets of paper and on a photocopier enlarge them to the size you want. Next, place your pattern pieces under a sheet of patchwork template plastic and carefully draw around the edges, copying your pattern to the plastic. Remember to allow at least a 1/4" seam allowance around the edge of each piece. Cut out the plastic and now you have a durable pattern with all the pieces necessary to make up your own bear design. (Double check them all for fit before marking out on your fur fabric. See Cross-checking for a perfect fit, page 37).

Grid System - Proportions

This is essentially a simple method to enable you to get the basics right when drawing your design out on paper. As with humans, teddy bears have a certain set of proportions, although they can vary a lot more than the human form. There are many different bears around and we are not talking just about size here but proportions of head to body and limbs for an overall look. Some bears can be quite extreme in their proportions and some are very traditional in form, yet they are all still instantly recognizable as teddy bears. Luckily we can take quite generous artistic license when designing our bears, but to start off with there are some useful generalizations to know. As with many artistic pursuits though, it is a case of learn the rules first and then you can break them.

As a teddy bear really is like a little animal in its own right, it "grows" along the same lines as other animals. That is, if you are thinking of a baby bear it will have a larger head and shorter muzzle than an adult. It might also have bigger eyes, shorter, thicker limbs and heavy paws. An older bear will have a smaller head, longer muzzle, bigger body and longer limbs (as in *Fig. 1*).

In general though, the main things to remember when either sketching out your bear freehand or drawing him within a grid system are that:

• Overall the height of your bear will be close to four
  head heights.
• The body is about twice as long (from neck to bottom) as
  the head is high (from crown to base of neck).
• The limbs are around 3/4 the length of the body, that is
  almost two head heights, or equal in length.
• The arms tend to be slightly longer than the legs. (This
  dates from the first Steiff bear designs in 1902/3, when
  they were initially sketched from real bears. They were
  therefore designed to stand on all fours, as well as to sit up
  in the characteristic teddy bear pose that we know today.)

To start your grid lines decide the overall height of your intended design and mark that length as a vertical line. If you plan on making a large bear and do not have a sheet of paper large enough to get the whole pattern out at once, then perhaps make him up half scale and double it on an enlarging photocopier afterwards.

Divide your line into equal quarters (*Fig. 1*). The top quarter rep-

Figure 1.

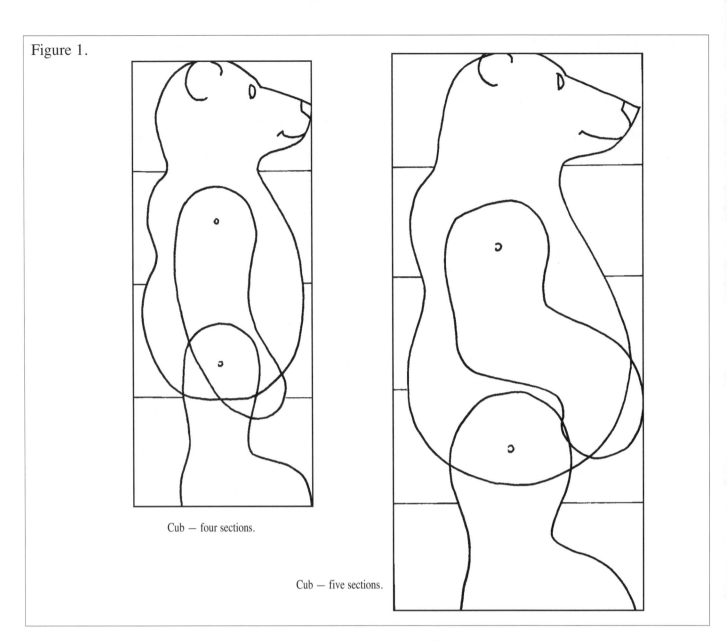

Cub — four sections.

Cub — five sections.

resents the head, the second measures the middle of the body, the third the base of the body and the last is the bottom of the feet. Remember that the legs will overlap the body to an extent, but will not quite reach the middle of the body. The arms can be drawn overlapping the body, or you may choose to take the measurements you have made for each quarter and draw the limbs separately.

Using these grid measurements you can draw in the outlines of your proposed bear from the front and on another set from the side and even the back should you wish. A front view will help you see where you may need to allow for darts to pull in and shape the sides of the body (*Fig. 2*), as well as gauge the width of the head gusset, and the relative size of the ears. If the bear has fairly straight sides to his body, you might try it as a two piece body pattern with darts for the top and bottom to pull in at the shoulders and hips. If the shape you are working with is rather

more complicated, say pear-shaped, you will need to make it up as a four-piece body. The extra side seams will be able to give you that extra shaping that you will need.

Once you are happy with your drawings, try them again in a sitting position to make sure you are happy with the length of legs and arms. Are the feet too far away from the body or too close? Do the arms lean nicely on the legs or floor, or are they too short when he is sitting down? Remember to add at least a 1/4" seam allowance around your finished lines before using your pattern.

For further details about head gussets and foot pads, see the relevant areas in the next section. Also make sure you cross-check your pattern to ensure that it all fits well together (see page 37).

Freehand designing — initial sketching
This is not as impressive as it sounds, so you need not be scared

16

off by it! It is merely using your knowledge of proportions without necessarily working "within the lines" of the grid system.

Start off by trying a little sketch or even doodle of how you want the finished bear to be. You might want him to sit or stand in a certain way, and there are bound to be certain strong characteristics which you want to bring out. Sketch him standing from the front and sitting from the side. This will give you something to refer back to in case you get bogged down with the details of designing.

Decide the finished height of your bear and make a note of it next to your sketches. Also note the age of the bear and any other unusual features you want to use. The size of the bear you want to make may be determined by a specific piece of fabric and the length of its pile. Using the same basic set of proportions from the Grid System you can now start designing your pattern. You may of course decide that you want to try something more extreme —

very long legs, for example. If so, just factor that into your overall equation for the proportions and divide up your measurement appropriately before you start. If you don't work out your proportions before you begin but just add on as you go, you may find that your finished bear is a lot bigger than you wanted. It may not fit your piece of fabric or even be too big for the length of fur that you had in mind for it!

Begin with the chosen size (a quarter or a fifth) of your overall measurement for the head. Now you can work on one piece at a time safe in the knowledge that all the pieces will fit together at the end. The main thing to remember is that your pattern is not WYSIWYG; that is, it is not really *"what you see is what you get"*. It takes a little practice to work out where you have to overcompensate your drawings to achieve the look you want. The hints given in the next section should help you sidestep such potential frustrations.

Figure 2.

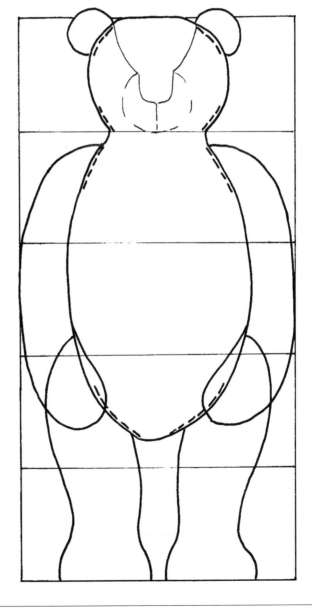

Cub — five sections.

⤚⟶ The Head ⟵⤙

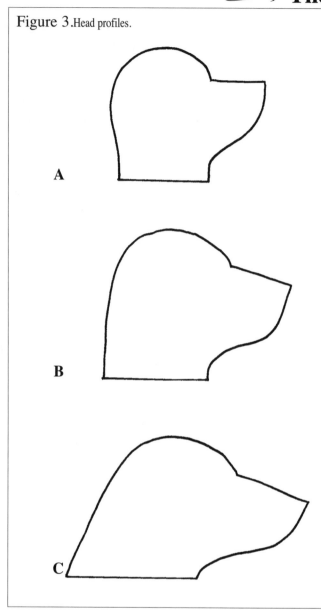

Figure 3. Head profiles.

Most teddy bears are made up using only three pieces in the head, which is quite astounding given the huge variety of bears which have been created using these same basic pieces. All the way through the design process at least two different examples will be given to show varying degrees of pattern design, but there is no reason why your bear should not be even more extreme than these. An old Steiff bear and a modern Pooh bear are good examples of quite different bears. The old Steiff is a classic design and one which is widely admired and emulated today, while the popular Pooh is a much more modern interpretation of a teddy bear and very different in character and pattern.

Neck length. With the height measurement which you have worked out for the bear you want to make, start with the side head piece and draw in a basic sort of shape. It may look something like one of the heads in *Fig. 3*. One of the most annoying things in a head pattern is when the neck joint ends up sitting right under the chin due to lack of neck fabric, so make sure you allow slightly more neck length than you think you will need. You will lose some of that length once you gather it up around the neck disc.

Basic head shape. If you are thinking of making a dressed bear you might want him to be a little more anthropomorphic than you would otherwise; that is, you might want him to look and pose in a more human fashion to suit his outfit. An upright stance would suit such a bear so his head might look more like *Fig. 3A* than *3C*. A more bear-ish looking bear would look better with a more naturalistic head shape such as *Fig. 3C*. Of course he might be more, or less, extreme than either of these.

Muzzle top line. Having made sure you have adequate neck length and having determined his overall "stance", now look at each angle and curve of the head piece and decide what you want to achieve with your pattern. The straight top line of the muzzle is a good place to start, *Fig. 4A-B*. On some patterns you will find that this line is curved downwards, but in general it is straight. This is probably because a drooping top line can make the head gusset harder to fit accurately. (A drooping line is great for a bunny pattern however, where of course the muzzle would also be short.)

A younger bear or a Pooh bear would have quite a short muzzle

line, whereas an older bear or an antique Steiff-style bear would have a long one. Remember that, like the neck length, you will lose some of the muzzle length when the head gusset piece is fitted in. The two side head pieces will curve together to meet at the point of the nose, so draw the muzzle line slightly longer than you expect you will want.

Muzzle angle. The angle of the muzzle line can also determine the tilt of the jaw. A level line will make a bear look straight ahead or even a little upward, depending on where his nose is embroidered. A line tilting downward will make a bear look down. This angle of the head can also be achieved by tilting the angle of the neck line (*Fig. 4C-D*). By having point C higher than point D, that is, the back of the neck shorter than the front, the muzzle win tilt upwards. Conversely, by having point C longer than point D, or the back of the neck longer than the front, the muzzle will point downwards.

Be cautious when using these methods to change the tilt of the head though, as a little change can give quite a dramatic result. Using one method or the other is really sufficient as both together can often be too extreme.

Depth of muzzle. Having determined the length of the muzzle with the top line (*Fig. 4A-B*) now have a look at the depth of the muzzle (B down to D). As before, you will be losing a bit of the depth when the seam A-D is sewn and the stuffing fills and rounds out the muzzle. Muzzle depth is important and if it is not there you may find that your bear looks more like a rat!

End of snout. You may want a very blunt muzzle on your bear (*Fig. 4A* halfway to D) in which case your line may be nearly vertical from the point of the nose down to the chin. An absolutely vertical line may result in more than a blocky snout, however. As mentioned before, the end of the muzzle has to curve around to meet the mid-point in the end of the head gusset. This means that some of the pointiness of the snout will be lost when the head is sewn. If your line A halfway to D starts off as vertical after sewing you may find that it now actually pulls back, giving more the appearance of a bull-dog than a bear! Generally, allow a little bit more of an angle to the point of the snout than you want to finish up with, as in *Fig. 4*, to give a more natural appearance.

Overall muzzle length. A simple rule of thumb (or nose in this case!) is that however long you make your bear's muzzle, it should not exceed the length of the rest of the head (*Fig. 5*). If it

does you will find that your bear is all nose and no head and looks rather unbalanced. Extremely long muzzles can work well provided they have head to balance them.

The eye spot. In *Fig. 4*, point B is the base of the muzzle where the forehead curves down to meet it. It is sometimes known as the "eye spot" because it is close to this point on the seam, (either just to the inside or the outside) that the eyes are set in. On some patterns there is no real definition between the muzzle and the forehead, and from point A to the crown of the head midway between B and C is a straight line. While this can give a certain look to the bear it can also cause some difficulties, mainly in the lack of a reference point. When used, this reference point or "eye spot" can be a great help for accurate pinning in and sewing of the muzzle, as well as providing a socket for the eye and giving extra definition to the forehead.

Forehead height. The shape of the crown of the head will depend largely on the curve you make (*Fig. 4B-C*). The old Steiff bears had large broad heads with not much height in the forehead. This means that the curve from the "eye spot" at point B to the crown of the head is very gradual and longer rather than higher. A baby bear or Pooh bear on the other hand has a much higher forehead, so the curve would be much higher and more domed. However you decide to have the shape of your bear's head, keep the curves smooth and regular and avoid odd humps or flat spots.

Neck opening size. Ideally the finished neck opening should snugly accommodate the neck joint without too much room to spare. For convenience the neck joint should also be the same size as the other four limb joints. (This is not always so, for example you may be working on a special design or animal such as a koala or rabbit which has larger legs than arms. It is always quicker if you can design your pattern to have five joints sets of equal size,

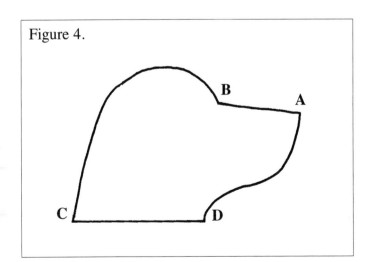

Figure 4.

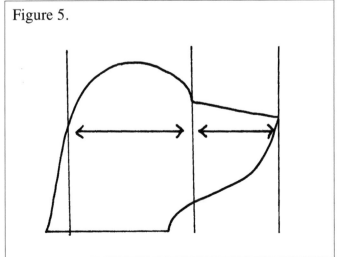

Figure 5.

however.) The finished size of the neck opening will depend on the length (*Fig. 4C-D*) of the two head pieces as well as the width of the end of the head gusset (*Fig. 7D-E*).

If the opening is too large for the joint you may find that you will end up with puckers or gathers around the base of the neck after you have pulled in the fabric around the base of the disc. If the opening is too small of course the joint may not fit in at all; or if you are using joint sizes that are too small the neck may look spindly and very thin. (Working out appropriate joint sizes for your pattern are covered in the section on limb design.)

As three pieces go into making up the neck opening it is important to achieve a balance between those three shapes. If for example, the back of the head comes down in a straight line or even curves in towards the base of the neck, your line (as in *Fig. 4C-D*) will be quite short. In that case it will be necessary to make the base of your head gusset piece (*Fig. 7D-E*) wider to compensate for it and to avoid a really skinny neck. It is interesting to note that a skinny neck also gives the effect of no cheeks, as there is little fabric to fill out there when stuffing.

If the back of your head looks more like *Fig. 3*, bear C, then the end of the head can afford to be narrower. In some bears you will see that the end of the head gusset actually finishes in a point. This can make pinning and sewing a little difficult and there is a potential for fraying of the fabric at the point, so perhaps you will find a narrow blunt end easier to work with than a point.

Sometimes the head gusset does not go all the way to the base of the neck but finishes at a point in the middle of the back of the head. If that is the case, then remember that the two side head pieces are going to have to give the shape to the back of the head by themselves, so allow a good base length to work with. (*Fig. 4C-D*)

Darts. Extra shape can be given to your bear's head by the use of darts, just as it can in dressmaking. *Fig. 6* shows some of the most common places where you may put darts in a head pattern. AR darts are sewn closed first and then the head is sewn together as normal. A small dart in the crown of the head at point A is occasionally used to give a little extra curve to the top of the head when viewed from the front.

Point B shows a dart (sometimes it is straight rather than angled) where inset ears can be sewn into the head before it is turned. This technique can be quicker than sewing the ears on after the head is finished and stuffed, but it also leaves no room for error or adjustment. If you use the sewn-in ear method and your sewing and stuffing are not entirely accurate you may find that your bear ends up with lopsided ears or with a look that you did not intend. It is probably a good idea when working on a new pattern to have the ears sewn on afterwards as then you can play around with the character of your bear and adjust the ears accordingly.

Point C in *Fig. 6* shows a dart at the base of the neck. This can

Figure 6.

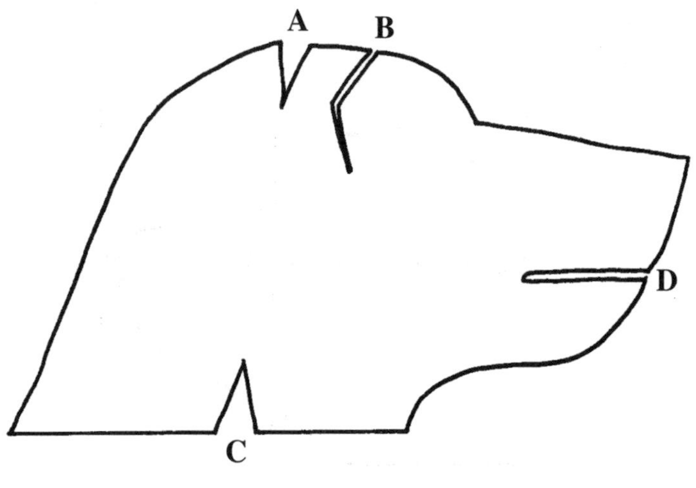

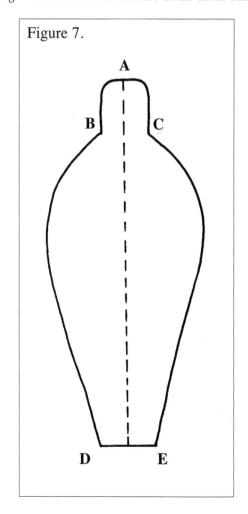

Figure 7.

help to not only reduce what would be a very large neck opening but it also can give some extra cheek shape. Just ensure that the dart does not extend up too far into the cheek area, otherwise you would be removing cheek shape rather than accentuating it.

Point D shows a slit in the mouth area which you would use if you wanted to make a bear with an open mouth. An oval shaped piece of fabric (pink felt or something suitable to show the inside of the mouth) is then folded in half and sewn into the slit. A good tip for retaining a good mouth shape when stuffing an open mouth head is to cut an oval of card slightly smaller than your mouth lining and place inside the head against the back of the felt before stuffing. This will prevent the mouth from curving open as the stuffing fills the muzzle.

⟳ Head Gussett ⟳

Of course, all of the characteristics and measurements that you have given your side head pieces need to correspond to the head gusset. As it is a symmetrical shape it can be drawn in half against the folded edge of your drawing paper or card. That way when you cut it out and open it up it will be perfectly symmetrical. If the gusset is slightly asymmetrical you may find that the head will be twisted or distorted when it is made up, so great care should be taken to keep it as perfect as possible.

Once again we will look at each line and curve separately and see how they all fit together.

Nose width. The width of the nose or muzzle across the top of the gusset relates to the depth of the muzzle that you have already drawn on the side head piece. There is no absolute rule regarding a suitable ratio of width to depth, but around 2/3 width to 3/3 depth seems to work well. If the nose on the head gusset is narrow and the muzzle is deep from the side, when it is made up the bear will look rather like *Fig. 8A*. This can sometimes be what you want, however, and it certainly works better than the opposite, of having a wide shallow muzzle giving you the result of *Fig. 9C*. This bear can look more like a duck-billed platypus than a bear! The 2/3 to 3/3 ratio will give you more of *Fig. 9B*, where the width is balanced by the depth giving a nicely rounded muzzle when viewed from the front.

Having measured the depth of your muzzle on your head piece

(*Fig. 4B* straight down to the bottom of the chin) take off 1/3 of the length and then divide it in half as your paper or card is doubled. Mark a spot that far in from the folded edge and use that as point B or C on *Fig. 7*, depending on which way you are working. This is your starting point for the head gusset shape.

Nose length. Using the length of the top muzzle line from your side head piece, (*Fig. 4A-B*) you can gauge the length of the nose on the head gusset. Of course, your new line will be shorter than the top muzzle line as the side head piece has to wrap around and meet the other side piece and a little more will be lost to the seam allowance. You can play around with this using a scrap of string the length of your top muzzle line, or you can sketch it roughly using that length as a guide and trim to fit when cross-checking your pieces.

Nose shape. Fig. 8 gives a variety of nose shapes for the head gusset. The end of the nose can be created in a variety of shapes, depending on the look you want to achieve. From A to E we have a square-ended blocky shape, a rounded end, a tapered cone-shaped end, a shovel-shaped end and a gently rounded slightly tapering end. In general the extremes of C and D are rarely used.

Head gusset width. Now that you have drawn in the desired nose on your head gusset you need to construct the shape of the rest of the head gusset (*Fig. 7B-D/C-E*). The length of the curve will match the length of the curve in the side head piece (*Fig. 4B-C*)

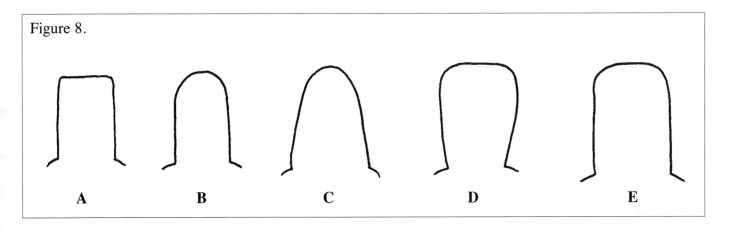

Figure 8.

A   B   C   D   E

and can be measured using a scrap of string or a flexible drafting curve. The drafting curve is also useful for drawing a nicely graduated curve if you have trouble with freehand sketching.

The shape of the curve you draw should relate in general to the corresponding section on the side head piece, in order to avoid puckering when sewing, but it does not have to be exact. In fact, if you are working towards that baby bear or Pooh bear style with a high rounded forehead, a narrower head gusset will work better and enhance the height of the forehead. Following an extreme brow curve in all three head pieces can result in a boxy look to the front of the head. The old Steiffs have broad heads which have been achieved by the use of a wide head gusset, but have very little height in the curve of the side head pieces.

The widest part of the gusset is usually at the midway point through the depth of the head (from the base of the muzzle at the eye spot to the back of the head). This can be judged accurately by referring to your side head piece, finding the half-way point and measuring the length of that curve from the eye spot to the top of the crown.

Gusset length. It is a good idea to allow a little extra in the length

of the head gusset as it can always be trimmed off when sewing the head, but it is annoying to find yourself just a little short. Sometimes the end of the head gusset is left long enough to become a flap which folds under the joint in the neck opening. The bolt or cotter pin of the jointing system pierces through the center of the flap. Instead of gathering around the opening it is then sewn shut using the three sides of the flap. This is an old technique which was sometimes used, as was the use of a disc of the fur fabric under the neck joint to close the neck instead of gathering.

Head pattern variations. There are quite a number of ways that the three piece head pattern can be cut into more pieces for additional special effects. In general the new parts are sewn together before sewing the head as normal (See Construction section on sewing). The oldest of these extra cuts would be the center seam on the head gusset.

Center seam head gusset. Historically this was used by Steiff in their early bear making years. As the head gusset was so wide it was sometimes split in two lengthwise with each half placed on either side of the fabric selvedge to economize on the mohair. If you want to try a center seam bear it is an easy thing to do, mere-

Figure 9.

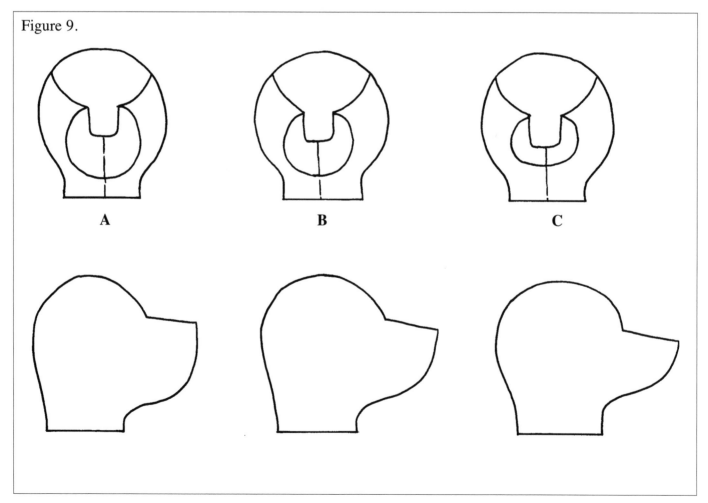

ly cut your head gusset in half down its length remembering to add on your seam allowance to each side. Sew the two halves together before sewing your head as normal.

The look that a center seam gives can be quite charming as it tends to pull down slightly giving an apple shape to the head. The direction of the fur can also be used to enhance this effect You might try having the fur heading away from the center seam on both sides, which would give the look of a center-part! This can be fun for a dressed or character bear.

Inset muzzle. The simplest form of this would be the cone-shaped nose achieved by using a circular piece of fabric with a pie-shaped wedge cut out of it. The wedge-shaped opening is then sewn shut creating a cone and this is stuffed and stitched onto a ball-shaped stuffed head. The nose is often in a shorter pile fabric or in a contrasting shade.

More commonly however, the inset muzzle is made like *Fig. 11*, where your initial design of a three piece head becomes a six-piece head by cutting off the muzzle. Remember to add your seam allowance to your cut edges and sew the muzzle tips back onto the relevant pieces before stitching up your head as normal.

There is no reason why the inset muzzle has to be sewn using straight lines. You may want to try making a bear with a curved inset muzzle, particularly with the head gusset piece, which can give a less abrupt transition between two different furs.

Using the inset muzzle is great if you want a different color on the nose from the rest of the head. If you are making a black bear, for example, a black nose and black eyes in a black face can make the whole face invisible. By using an inset muzzle in a brown or gold you can highlight the face and add some great accents to the black bear. (In real life black bears often do have a lighter color around the face.)

Different effects can be achieved depending on whether all three head pieces are inset with another color or whether only the sides are inset. There is no reason why the muzzle should be only a lighter color on a dark or black bear. The muzzle could be a darker color on a lighter bear for contrast, or even a shorter pile length. Different fabrics can also be used, for example leather, suede, ultrasuede or velvet will all create very different looks.

You might try experimenting with using only inset muzzle sides (*Fig. 11A*) but leaving the head gusset intact. This can produce a very gentlemanly look, especially when the fur used on the sides is longer than the rest of the head, giving your bear long moustaches.

There are other ways of using inset muzzles which require incorporating different materials and techniques in with your mohair or synthetic fur fabrics. Porcelain, carved wood, molded felt, fragrance-impregnated clay, modeled Fimo or resin compounds can all be used to create bear faces with great character. Polymer clays are popular as they are easy to model and can be fired in a domestic oven instead of a special kiln. Often a molded rim around the face is left so that the head fur can then be glued to it. A face "mask" can even be formed as an underlay, with the fur then laid over and glued onto it to give extra shaping to the head. Sculpted and hinged jaws with tongues and teeth can also be set into a fur-covered muzzle.

Think of the look you want to achieve with your bear, and then experiment with different techniques. You are only limited by your imagination!

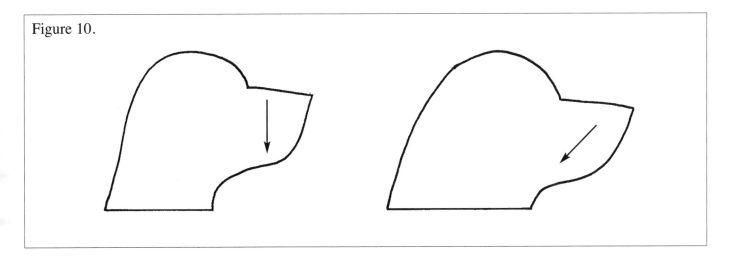

Figure 10.

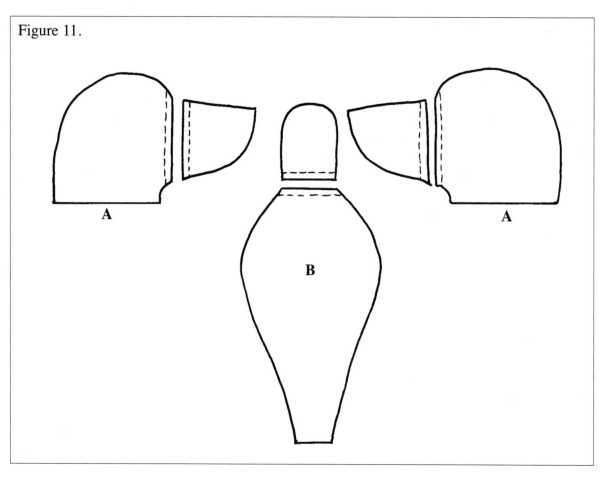

Figure 11.

⟵ Ears ⟶

Ears are a simple shape and may be found in a number of subtle styles, as in *Fig. 12*. The arrows indicate fur direction, which goes out and off the edge of the ears giving a soft and natural look. Four ear pieces go into making two ears and the pieces are usually symmetrical. You might like big ears or small ears; both can work equally well but will give very different looks. The shape of the ears you choose will depend on the style of bear you are working towards. The ear shape in *Fig. 12A* has a short base and once it is curved and sewn on to the head the edges will actually pull in giving an almost circular appearance. While this look may be a little extreme for a traditional bear it would certainly suit a Pooh type bear or a panda where little ears sit up high on the head.

The conical shape of *Fig. 12B* would give a more doggy appearance, while *Fig. 12C* is more of a classic shape and would suit an old Steiff style bear. A wider base means that you have more fabric to curve when positioning the ear on the head, and it can give a more natural look. (See more about ears and their placement in the Construction section on ears.)

The base of the ear may also be shaped instead of flat. *Fig. 12D*

shows an ear with a concave curve and *Fig. 12E* shows one with a convex curve. If you have not used an ear with a curved base before, experiment using scraps of leftover fur and see how they shape up when pinned on to a tennis ball or a grapefruit. The curved lower edges can give quite different effects and one might be just the look that you are after.

Fig. 12F shows a one-piece ear. This is often used in miniature bear making where the ear pieces are very tiny. The circle is folded in half and the ear is sewn completely shut. A slit is then made along the flat edge (but not all the way to the corners) and the ear is turned through. While this technique works well with miniature fabrics such as upholstery velvet or with short pile mohair which stands straight up, there is a problem in using it with fur that has a definite direction. As you can see from the direction of the arrow in *Fig. 12F*, while the fur will be going the right way (up) for one side of the ear, it will be going the wrong way (down) for the other side.

Whichever ear style you settle on remember to allow enough depth to the ear for a comfortable turn-under once it is sewn and turned right side out.

COMPLETION OF THE HEAD PATTERN

Having now designed our pieces for the head, we need to double-check that they fit together perfectly before committing ourselves to marking and cutting out the fabric. It is also a good idea to mark an arrow on the pieces to indicate fur direction. Fur direction is generally down or diagonally back from the point of the nose, see *Fig. 10*.

While they are still in paper or scrap card form, these pieces can be checked and trimmed down if necessary. (See Cross-checking for a perfect fit, page 37.) If you have not already done so, remember to add at least a 1/4" seam allowance around the edge of your pattern pieces.

From the head we can now work down to the body. Double the measurement you used for the height of the head and make that the overall length of the body. Now you are ready to start designing your bear's torso.

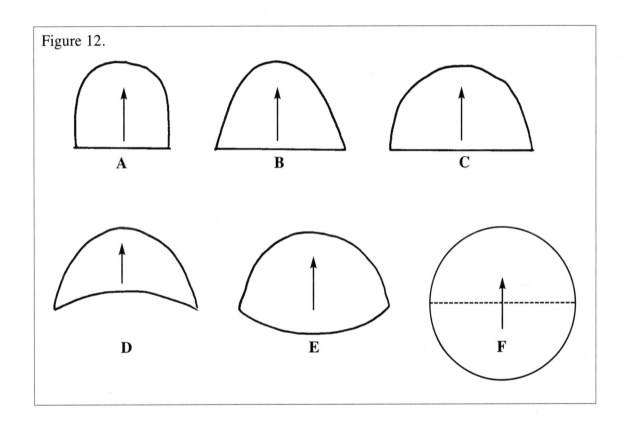

Figure 12.

⤳ **The Body** ⤳

Perhaps you have forgotten the details you wanted to show in your bear's form, so check those initial sketches and doodles you made. Humps, sway backs, big bottoms, tummies, chests and posture are all things which need to be considered. Is your bear to be fat or thin, extra-long bodied or perhaps chunky in build? If he or she is to be dressed or rather small would a simpler two-piece body be adequate? Is the neck joint to be sitting flat giving an upright posture or perhaps angled forward and down to give a slumped appearance and poor posture?

Take time to think about all the things you want to express in your bear's body. We will start with a four-piece body pattern as in *Fig. 13A* (that is two tummy parts and two back parts which all join together) and then also look at the two-piece body (*Fig. 13B*).

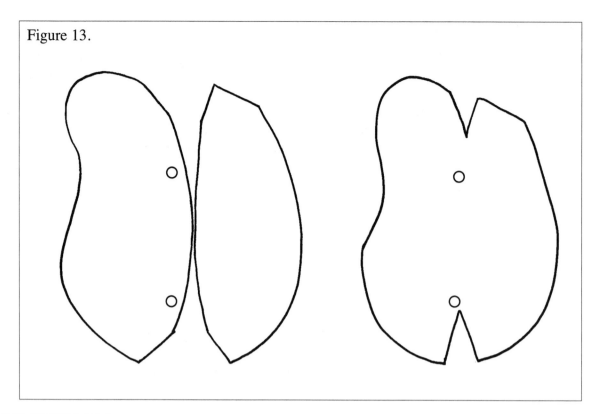

Figure 13.

THE FOUR-PIECE BODY

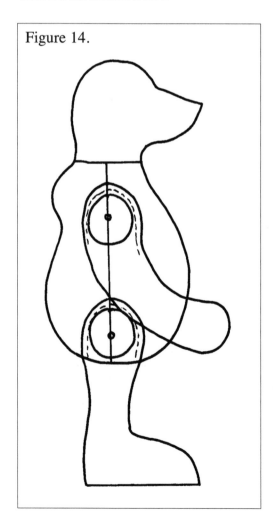

Figure 14.

There are a few things to keep in mind as you design your four-piece body. Of course the length and side seam shape of the front and back pieces have to match exactly, but this can be checked using the next section "Cross-checking for a perfect fit." This is really the fine tuning of the design process and can be left till last.

Ignore the limbs for the moment, as they will follow on from the body design. Remember that you will want the limbs to be balanced down the midline of the body, when viewed from the side (See *Fig. 14*). This will help determine where the joint spots should be marked. In general the midline of the body will closely correlate to its side seams, meaning that the front and back halves of the body will be quite well-matched in width across the pieces. This also means that the joint marks are usually close to the side seam edges, but not on them.

If the back of the body is much fatter than the front (*Fig. 15A*) but the joint spots are still close to the seams, you will end up with a bear with a hunched over appearance as his arms will be positioned close together on the front of his chest. Conversely, if you have more tummy than back in your pattern pieces (*Fig. 15B*) the side seam will be closer to his back. Should you have the joint spots close to those seams he will appear to be all chest and no back.

There is no reason why the arm and leg joint spots have to be on the same body piece all the time. You may be aiming for a particular look and might find that if the arm spots are slightly forward, that is on the tummy piece, while the leg spots are on the back piece you can get the pose you are aiming for.

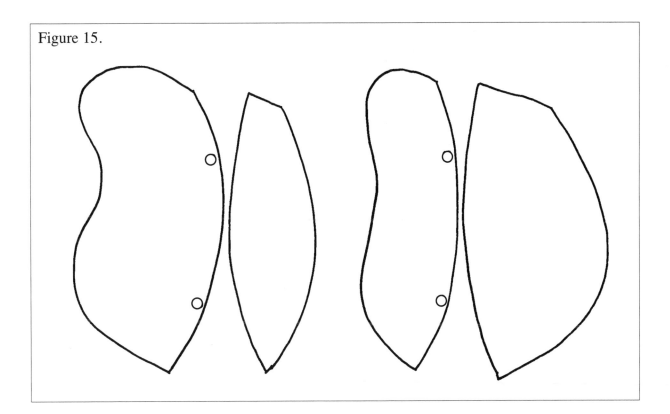

Figure 15.

THE BACK PIECE

Draw in a rough boxy shape to delineate the back of the body using the measurement you have calculated (double the height of the head, or perhaps more if you are working on a long-bodied bear). As with the head we will look at each curve separately.

The neck. This is the flat part where the neck of the head will join onto the body (*Fig. 16A-B*). If you want the neck joint to sit flat you would keep this section fairly level but if you want the head to tilt slightly down or forward you might tilt the angle down towards the side seam. The body's finished neck section (A-B plus H-I) may look somewhat thicker than the base of neck on the head pattern but that is fine. The fabric can be gathered around the neck disc in the body to ensure a snug fit.

The hump. Continue from your neck line to his hump (*Fig. 16B-C*). Traditionally the early Steiff bears had quite large humps. Drawn from real life, these humps are actually the bears' shoulder blades which stick up higher than his back when he walks. If you are designing a modern bear or perhaps a bear, which you intend to dress, then you might not want a hump on your pattern at all.

A good hump tends to go out rather than up in its curve. A high hump may mean that the head ends up being pushed forward and the bear may look hunchbacked. A narrow hump can end up looking a little pointed and mean, so keep your curve well rounded.

The "*backbone*". Many bear patterns have a straight back, but this is your chance to add a little extra life into your bear. Most four-legged animals do have rather flat backs, unless you are thinking of an old sway-backed horse, but the teddy bear is no ordinary animal! He is really designed to sit upright so consequently he often has a curve to his back, which balances, out his bottom. (*Fig. 16C-D*) shows where his spine may curve to fit his posture. For a dressed bear, particularly a female, you would want some waist and this curve to the back will help achieve that.

The bottom. A bear spends a lot of its time sitting down so it needs a good base to sit on. If it does not have one it may tend to tip over backwards instead of holding its pose. Continue with your line and curve it down to the full length of the body (*Fig. 16D-E*). This curve might be more pronounced than you intended, as point E will meet up with point K after the dart E-F-K is sewn together in the side seam. Do not worry about it at this stage as it can be corrected if necessary when the pieces are cross-checked. At this stage it is better to have too much bottom than not enough as it can be easily trimmed back.

The darts. The dart at the top of the body (A-G-H) pull in to form the shoulders and dart E-F-K at the bottom of the body pull in to form the hips. Without darts of some sort the body would look rather boxlike on a four-piece pattern and flat on a two-piece pattern. As well as giving a better shape to the body, the darts enable the arms and legs to sit well on the torso.

Darts on the body pieces do not usually go into the body any deeper than the joint spots for the limbs. The more acute the angle of the darts the more fabric you have removed, therefore the more exaggerated the angle that you will create.

The side seam. Continuing up from the dart at point F, the last thing to do in designing your back body piece is to create the side seam. With a four-piece body the main advantage is that you have the chance to shape the sides of the body, something which you cannot do in a two-piece pattern. A straight line is what you would get down the side of a two-piece body, so that is not usually done when working on a four-piece pattern such as this. A gentle convex curve is often used, but if you want a bear with a nipped-in waist you might even try a slightly concave curve as this would remove fabric from the waistline.

The openings. The main opening for the body will be in the back section. It is where the completed body will be turned through, jointed, stuffed and closed. This opening will need to be accessible to all five joints so it is usually placed midway down the back. Marking it on your pattern, together with the fur direction (downwards) help remind you until such things become second nature.

The joint spots. Another good reminder to place joint spots on your new pattern. It may seem silly at first, because you really are not sure where the limbs will go at this stage. If you mark a spot for the legs close to the edge and just up from the inner end of the lower dart, and one for the arms close to the edge but just down from the inner end of the upper dart, you will give yourself an important reference point.

When it comes to placing the limbs on your newly made bear for the first time, if you have no marks to guide you then it will be up to guesswork and luck to get them level. Passing long needles through the body to try and find a level might help but more often than not your bear may end up with a touch of scoliosis! If you are lucky and get it right, then you may still have problems the next time you want to make up that pattern.

If the reference points are already marked inside the body of your bear you can check them to see if they are correct by pushing a pin through the spot from the inside and holding the jointed limb against it from the outside. If the limb needs to be perhaps 1/8in (.31cm) higher or lower than the mark then you can easily match that on the other side of the body. Even more importantly, you can then go straight back to your pattern and correct the mark on the pattern template so that from then on that pattern will be perfect every time. (More on finding the right position for the limbs in the Construction section.)

THE TUMMY PIECE

Now that you have the back half of the body already designed, the front becomes very easy. Match the overall length and thickness of the back piece.

The neck. The width of the neck (*Fig. 16H-I*) on the tummy piece should equal that on the back piece, so the first part of the tummy piece is simple to work out. The angle you chose for the back (A-B) should also line up and continue once the side seams and darts are sewn, so draw your line (H-I) at roughly the same angle. It will pull down in the center a little once the darts (A-G-H) are sewn together so you might want to compensate for that.

The chest. The top half of the chest is normally fairly flat (I-J) as it slopes down towards the tummy. If you make this line too convex a curve you may find that your bear ends up with a "pouter pigeon" chest which in extreme cases may even touch his chin. Even if you desire a tubby bear don't make him too fat above the middle of his tummy or it will not look very natural.

The tummy. Here (J-K) is where your bear can become plump if you want him to. Finish his tummy off with a nice curve down to point K. Too heavy a curve can result in a boxy shape to the lower part of his tummy.

The darts. As with the back pattern piece, the darts A-G-H and E-F-K help to shape the contours of your bear's body. They need to match perfectly so copy them from the back piece by flipping your paper over and drawing it in reverse against the edge of the tummy piece. If you have been using thick card and cannot see through it, draw just the dart lines on some tracing paper or even thin writing paper and flip that over to use it.

You have now designed the two halves of your body and it is time to check the pattern before copying it onto a permanent template using the "Cross-checking for a perfect fit" section.

THE TWO-PIECE BODY

If you have decided that a four-piece body is really not necessary for what you are trying to achieve in your design, then a two-piece body will do. Miniaturists often use the two-piece body, and it is also useful for small bears and many other larger styles.

The basic aspects of design are the same as those for the four-piece body. The only thing that is missing is the side seam The shaping of the sides of the body is done using the darts only to pull in the shoulders and hips (*Fig. 13B*). If designing a two-piece body, you can follow the previous guidelines for a four-

piece one, omitting the section on the side seams but using the darts at the top and bottom.

You can also take your favorite four-piece body pattern and make it into a two-piece by overlapping the back and tummy sections at the side seams until only the darts remain. This is sometimes useful when you want to reduce a four-piece pattern down to a fairly small size, say 4in (10cm)- 6in (15cm), where a two-piece body will be less awkward to sew.

BODY PATTERN VARIATIONS

There is no reason why your body pattern need be limited to either two or four pieces. If there is a complicated shape that you are trying to achieve or if you need to use more than one color in the body (as, for example in a panda), you will need to further divide up your pieces. Pattern Two given in this book, The Wild Bear Cub, gives an example of this with an inset chest of a second color. Pattern Three, The Dressed Bear, also shows what can

be done by cutting up the body and limb patterns and using different fabrics to make a bear with a sewn-in costume.

These are just a couple of examples of what can be done by pushing the boundaries of your design. Experiment with your patterns and have fun with them. New techniques and styles are often discovered through such experiments!

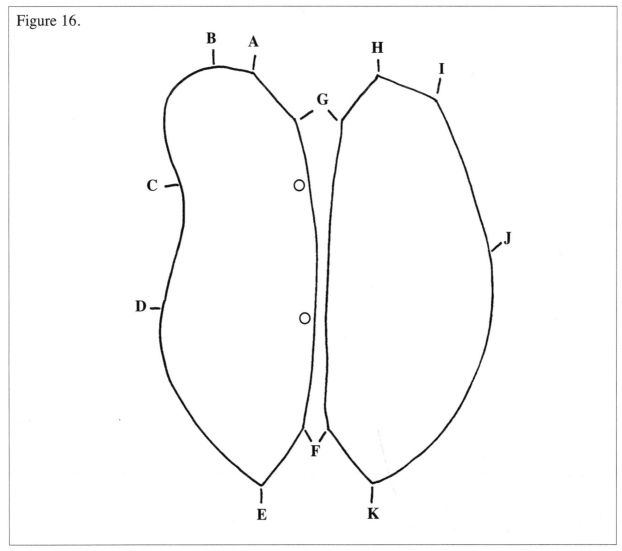

Figure 16.

THE LIMBS

You have already ensured that the body will not be too small for the head with your calculations, and this will in turn enable the limbs to fit nicely onto the body. There should always be enough room on the body for a good space between the base of the neck and the top of the shoulder, and between the top of the thigh and the armpit, otherwise the limbs will look crowded on a too small body. Similarly, not only is adequate length a concern but also adequate depth through the body. If the body is too thin there might be no room for chest or back between the arms, or for tummy or bottom between the legs. If you want to make a thin bear remember to scale down the thickness of the limbs to keep him in proportion. At the other end of the scale, a really tubby bear will look odd if his arms and legs are stick thin so he may need to have his limbs plumped up a little.

Limb length to body. Your initial measurement for the length of the limbs will be roughly three-quarters or even equal the length of the body. The same guideline still holds when working with bent limbs, measuring from the tip of the paw or the footpad straight to the top of the limb and ignoring the elbow or knee. If you shorten a bent limb to compensate for the fact that if it was straightened out it would be much longer, it tends to give a cramped look. When working on a pattern with two different arms or legs you may have to shorten the bent limb slightly otherwise it will look long in comparison to the straight one but even then you might find that it is more a case of artistic license than being anatomically correct.

Arm length to leg. As mentioned earlier, the ratio of arm to leg is close but the arm is often slightly longer than the leg. This extra length can give the arm a nice relaxed appearance, as when the bear is sitting the lower edge of the paw will rest on the "floor" from the wrist. The extra length of the arm is maybe only half a paw pad longer than the leg, so there is not that much difference particularly as the wrist is usually bent, which visually shortens the overall appearance of the arm.

⟾ The Arms ⟾

There are quite a few different ways to design your bear's arms (See *Fig. 17*); but basically you will choose either a one-piece arm which is folded over or a two-piece arm, where the inner and outer halves are separate. Which style you choose depends on what shape of arm you want.

The one-piece straight arm. (*Fig. 17A*). This is probably one of the most common arm styles and it is also the earliest, as Steiff used this pattern for their first bears. It is a nice traditional shape and it has the advantage of not having a seam down the visible front of the arm. There are limits however, to the variety of shapes which can be achieved with this one-piece pattern.

Because the main part of the arm is folded there is a limit as to the bend which can be given to it. The main change in position comes from lifting the angle of the wrist, as in the dotted line at A in *Fig. 18*. The wrist can be lifted to be in alignment with the wrist line of the paw pad on the other half of the arm, but no further.

There can also be some inherent weaknesses in the design of the straight one-piece arm There is an inner corner of the paw pad to be sewn in, and this corner is under stress when the arm is turned and stuffed. The result can be visible stitches in the corner or even the edge of the paw pad poking out. One solution to this problem is to cut a short slit up the corner in alignment with the fold of the arm (*Fig. 18C*). By taking the paw pad stitching past the corner and running it off to the folded edge you will ensure that the corner of the pad is well stitched down.

Another potential problem is the shape of the top of the shoulder (the same applies for the top of the thigh on the one-piece leg). The top of the limb needs to be well-rounded, especially at point B in *Fig. 18* where there should be a good indentation. If there is not, or if the sewing does not follow a good curve, then there is a chance that a corner will appear at the front of the shoulder (and the back of the thigh) when the piece is turned and stuffed.

To avoid this, always make sure that the limbs you are designing have a nice symmetrical curve to the tops of them. Exaggerate it if necessary to ensure that your sewing will have to follow down into that curve and run off into the folded edge, rather than cut across it (*Fig. 19A*).

Openings. Many teddy bear manufacturers leave the limb openings at the top, essentially creating a tube to be filled and jointed. This is because they usually use stuffing machines, which work like a vacuum cleaner in reverse, blowing the stuffing down a tube into the empty casing. The openings are then closed by hand over the top curve. The problem with closing over a curve, whether convex or concave, is in keeping the stitches neat and unpuckered and ensuring that the stuffing is smooth and round underneath.

Figure 17.

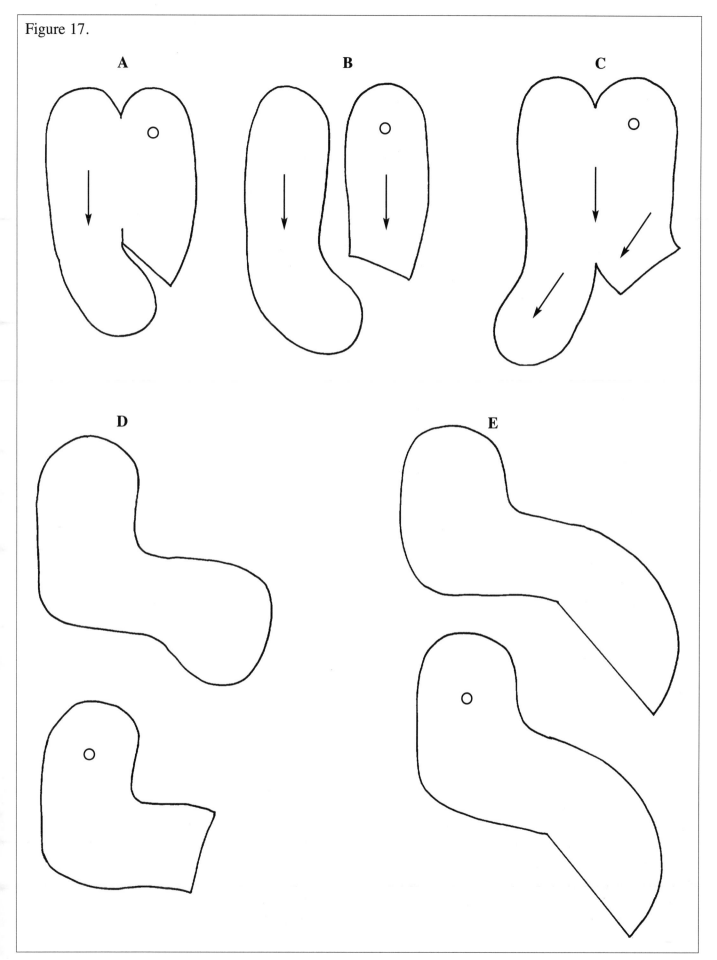

As a maker of hand-made bears you have the chance to improve on some techniques of mass production and take that bit of extra care and extra time to ensure that your work is of the highest possible quality. If you find that a commonly used technique just doesn't work for you or give you the finish you want then find your own solution, even if it means that it may be a little more time consuming. This book is all about finding out what works for you.

If a closing seam on the top of the limbs works well for you, then you are already giving that bit of extra care to your bear. You may find however, that a closing seam on a straight edge is much easier to work with and gives a much more invisible closure. It can also enable you to pack evenly and easily into the top curve of the limb. *Fig. 19B* shows where the opening would go in this case. The opening needs to give access to the joint as well as to the rest of the limb, so it begins at a point level with the joint marker and is at least as large as the disc intended for the joint.

Joint size and position. How do we determine the size and position of the joint discs at this stage? It is actually very simple. The seam allowance needs to be included in your drawing at this stage, even if just temporarily. If the seam allowance will extend outside the lines that you are drawing, then your lines are already defining the inner edge of your seam allowance. If your seam allowance will actually be inside your pattern lines (that is, you have already allowed for it in your overall size calculations), then draw a dotted line 1/4" inside your top curve of the shoulder as in *Fig. 19*.

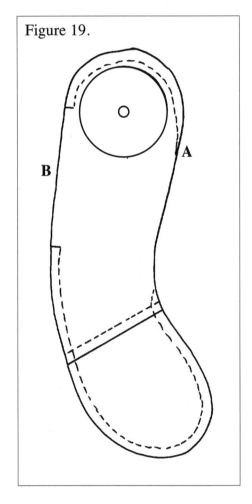

Figure 18.

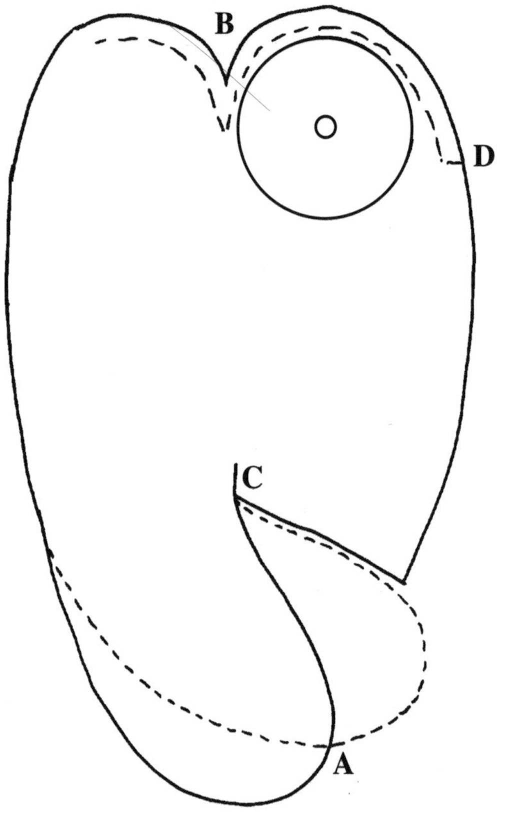

Figure 19.

It is important that the joint is a good size and fits fairly snugly into the curve that you have drawn. If the disc size is too small in relation to the limb, or if it is placed too low in the limb it will appear rather like the arm in *Fig. 20A* when it is stuffed and finished. The result is a bulbous shoulder that does not sit well combined with an arm that tends to pull out sideways instead of sitting firmly against the body and merely rotating forwards and backwards when moved.

A joint disc of a suitable size placed well within the curve of the shoulder will produce the more natural looking arm in *Fig. 20B*. It will also move as it should and not wobble. Finding the right size is easy. You have already worked out your seam allowance, giving you the inside space of your shoulder. With a compass draw a circle which is about 1/4in (.65cm) down from the inside seam edge but which otherwise fills the space, as in *Fig. 19*. That extra 1/4" of room between the inside seam edge and the outer

Figure 20.

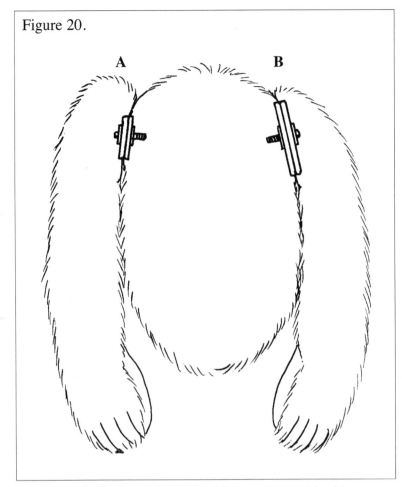

edge of the disc is all you need to be able to stuff around it without giving the shoulder a puffy look.

Make sure that your disc is centered with an equal amount of room all around the top curve. Where the point of your compass has been is where the joint mark will go. Measure across the circle you have made and you have exactly the size of the joint disc that you will need to make your bear.

If your joint mark is not exactly centered you may give yourself problems when you come to stuffing the bear. With the mark a little to the front of the arm you will find that the arm tends to pull across the body or twist the paw pad palm down instead of holding it upright. If the mark is a little back the arm can pull back and twist the paw out. The same thing applies to the legs so always make sure that your patterns are as accurate in their details as possible.

Shaping the arm and pad. The arm tends to taper down slightly from the shoulder to the wrist and then comes out into the curve of the paw. The paw pad itself can be any one of a variety of shapes from round to oval to spoon-shaped or long and thin. You might even want your bear to have thumbs!

Remember that if you are making a small bear with very large paws and very narrow wrists you may have trouble turning the paw through. The same thing can happen with big feet and narrow ankles (think about bunnies and kangaroos!). There are special tools which you can use to help you in such tight spots, see the Essential Tools section.

Once you are happy with the shape of your arm the shape of the paw pad can be determined by folding the arm in half. Before cutting out the whole arm, first cut out the longer outer arm leaving a wide edge around the shorter side. Then fold the arm in half so that the dip of *Fig. 18*, point B matches up with the slit at point C. Now the inner arm can be cut out using the outer arm as a guide to guarantee its symmetry.

When the arm is cut out in its folded state the shape of the paw pad is readily apparent. The angle of the wrist line on the inner arm can be changed to lengthen or shorten the paw pad if necessary.

Paw pad seam allowances. It is common to allow your normal seam allowance to every piece of the body, including the paw pads. The result of a seam allowance along the wrist of the paw pads is a straight arm and paw, as in *Fig. 21B*. If you allow too much seam allowance, or seam narrower than you had intended, the extra length of the pad (even though it might be very slight) can give the arm a turned out appearance as in *Fig. 21C*. This can also happen if you are working with a stretchy paw pad fabric such as some leathers.

If you do not allow for a seam allowance on your paw pads, however, you get an interesting result. You will need to ease in the slightly longer outer arm along the curve of the paw pad when you pin and sew it, but because the inner arm is slightly shorter than the outer arm, the paw pad tends to curve slightly inwards giving a natural look to the paw and an extra bit of shaping to the arm.

The two-piece straight arm. *Fig. 17B*. This style of arm is commonly found in commercial patterns. It does have the advantage of avoiding the weak corner problem of the paw pad in the one-piece arm, but it has the disadvantage of giving a visible seam to the front of the arm. It also involves extra sewing down a seam which may not be necessary. If you want to create a straight arm, try both techniques and decide for yourself which suits you better.

When designing a two-piece arm, draw the outer half first. That way, once you have worked out the shape you want, you can then easily get a perfectly matching inner arm by tracing over it. On the second arm, mark where you want the wrist of the paw pad and also mark the joint hole.

The one-piece bent arm. *Fig. 17C.* This is also sometimes called the "back-to-front arm". As you can see the paw is facing away from the arm instead of towards it as on the arm in *Fig. 17A.* The main advantage here is that the wristline of the paw pad on the inner arm is totally separate from the outer arm, eliminating that annoying paw pad corner problem. The design also means that you can have a bent arm in one piece as it is only joined from shoulder to the elbow. Because the paw on the outer arm is free from the proximity of the wrist line on the inner arm, there is much more flexibility in drawing your paw size and shape.

The disadvantage to this arm design is in the fur direction. Usually the direction of the fur on the arm is down towards the tip of the paw (see *Fig 17, A-E*). As the arrows indicate on *Fig. 17C* the fur would be going the right way on the outer side of the arm but the wrong way on the inner arm. On a short pile fur that stood straight up, however, this would not be a problem so perhaps you might find this a good design for a smaller bear pattern.

The two-piece bent arm with the paw pad facing in. *Fig. 17D.* The two-piece bent arm is a more modern interpretation of the teddy bear, but it is a design, which can give a lot of freedom and flexibility to the pose of your bear. If you are thinking about using bent limbs in your design, maybe you don't need them for all four limbs. You could have a bear with bent legs and straight

arms, or bent arms and straight legs. Perhaps you only want the bear to be holding something in one arm, such as a cub or a bunch of berries if you are working on a naturalistic design, or maybe a toy or a basket of flowers. In that case you may only need to have one bent arm and the other could be straight.

The bend of the arm can be made to suit whatever pose you intend the bear to hold, but remember to give him an elbow as just a curved arm can look rather "boneless"! The paw can bend down at the wrist, be straight or even bend up and the shape of the paw pad itself can be as varied as you want it to be.

The openings for bent arms and legs need to provide access to the joints as well as to the far corners of the paws and toes. *Fig. 22A* shows a suitable place to have the opening where it is on as straight an edge as possible, yet where it provides easy access to the joint as well as the paw. If the opening was left at either point B or C stuffing and jointing would be made more difficult.

The two-piece bent arm with the paws facing down. *Fig. 17E.* This is also known as the Steiff Teddy Baby style, after a design that Steiff first produced in the 1930s. The paw pad on this design is set in underneath the two matching halves of the arm, rather in the same way as the foot pad is set in on the leg.

Similarly, as a lot of the length of the foot is taken up with the curve of the footpad, it is necessary to allow quite a lot of length for the paw in this design when shaping the paw pad. Your inner and outer arms will look identical except for the fact that the inner half will have the joint spot marked on it.

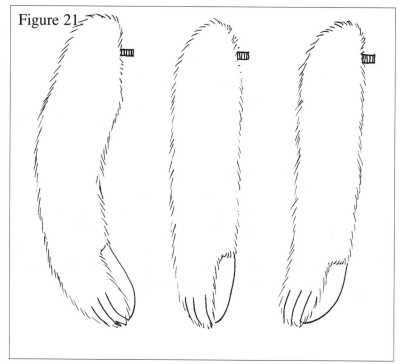

Figure 21.

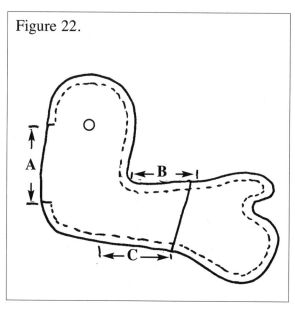

Figure 22.

The Legs

From the body length and the arm length you will have calculated the length of leg you want. You may be working towards a quite extreme design, for example a Pooh type bear has very short legs for his body length, or a more classic design like an early Steiff style bear which has legs about equal in length to the body, but slightly shorter than his arms.

Limb correlation. In order to keep your pattern consistent it is a good idea to match the shoulder and thigh curves at the top of the arms and legs. Not only does this make the designing of the legs much easier it means that you can use the same disc size on your joints and achieve a more balanced look.

As covered in the arm section it is a good idea to make sure that the top curve of your thigh is nicely rounded. This is especially important if you are working with a one-piece leg, in order to avoid corners appearing at the inside edge of the curve when your leg is turned through. By exaggerating it a little bit you will remind yourself to follow down into the curve with your sewing and run that seam off into the fold of the leg (see *Fig. 24A*).

The placing of the openings, and finding the joint size and position is the same as for the arms and should be easy to determine. If you have decided to have your openings on a straight side edge for the arms, then you can do the same for the legs. Your markings for the joint hole can be quickly transferred directly from your arm drawings, just as the shape of the top curve can be copied.

You then have to decide what style of leg would suit your bear best. There are as many leg styles as arms and there is no reason why the legs should necessarily match the arms. You may have designed two-piece bent arms but want the bear to have straight legs, so a one-piece pattern may suit.

Generally the arms and legs have a similar thickness or bulk in order to visually balance each other and matching up the top curve from the arms to the legs helps keep the limbs in relation to each other. The narrowing for the ankles is often reflected in the shape of the wrists, and the width is roughly the same for both.

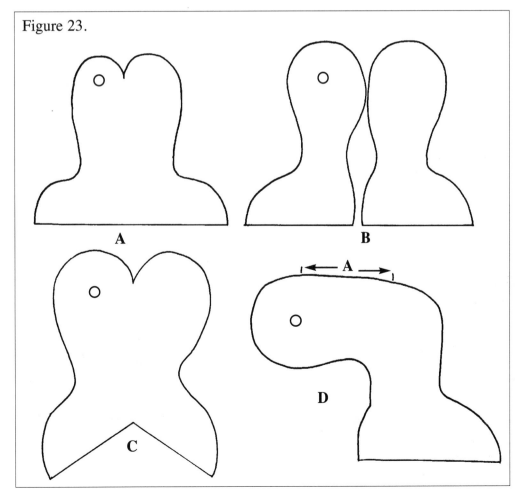

Figure 23.

A

B

C

D

Ankle shape. The shape of the ankle can be quite an abrupt corner (as in *Fig. 23A*) or a gentler curve (as in *Fig. 24*). You may find that the ankle can pull up when the leg is turned through, resulting in a foot where the toes are pulled back towards the body. In order to avoid this; try clipping the curve of the ankle after it is sewn (taking care not to cut all the way through to the seam) and before you turn it.

This is a common dressmaking technique to stop fabric from pulling or puckering around curves. Merely cut small wedges out of the fabric edge about 1/4in (.65cm) apart in the area you are concerned about.

Toe shape. The point of the toe can be either abrupt (as in *Fig. 23A*) or come down at more of an angle (as in *Fig. 24*). As the curve at the toe of the footpad will round out the toe of the foot it will give the effect of pulling in the toe. If the toe shape is almost vertical to begin with, you may find that the footpad will end up pulling the foot in at the toe, giving a club foot appearance.

This is a similar problem to the one covered with the shape of the end of the muzzle and fitting in the head gusset. Once again it is important to allow for the fact that your pattern pieces have to fit around curves and the shape you design is not necessarily the shape you will see when the pieces are sewn. If you plan to have a very large footpad, especially if it is a very wide one, remember to allow for it not only lengthwise but also in extending the point of the toe.

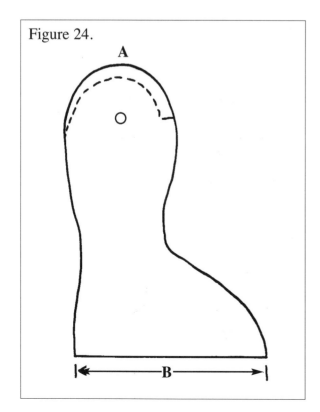

Figure 24.

A

B

Depth of the foot. There are no rules about the depth of the foot but if it is too deep the end result may look like a boot more than a foot, and if it is too shallow it may end up looking more like a duck's foot! Generally, about half the length of the foot is a good measurement for the depth.

Shape of the footpad. Historically the earliest teddy bears had either long, narrow footpads (Steiff) or pointed oval footpads (Ideal), and in manufactured bears the feet have tended to become shorter and rounder over the years. This is particularly true for the English bears.

The shape and size of the footpad can vary enormously and it depends on what you want. Bears can have any foot shape, from round, to oval to teardrop or even kidney bean. They can also be the same width from the toe to heel or have narrow toes and fat heels, or fat toes and narrow heels. You may find that your tastes will change with time. Perhaps you always thought that a long, narrow footpad was your style until you tried an offbeat asymmetrical shape. Don't stick with one "safe" shape, experiment and see how your look will change to fit it.

Calculating the fit of the footpad. Once you have drawn the straight bottom line to your foot you have decided on the length of the foot and can now calculate the exact size for the footpad. If you are working with a one-piece leg, double the measurement you have for the base of the foot (*Fig. 24B*) and deduct 1/2in (1cm) or 12mm which is twice your seam allowance for the seam at the toes. If you are working on a two-piece leg, find your base measurement and double it and then deduct 1in (3cm) or four times the seam allowance for the seam at the heels and the toes.

The measurement that you are left with is the circumference of your footpad. With a piece of string the same length and a sheet of waste cardboard which has some glue on it, you can play around with the shape of the foot. A pipe cleaner cut to the correct length and bent into a loop can also be a good way of working out the footpad shape, as can plastic coated electrical wire.

Once you have the rough dimensions and shape that you want, transfer it to a paper pattern. (If you are working on an asymmetrical foot, take the height and width measurements and draw in the curves according to the shape of your model). For a symmetrical footpad, fold a piece of paper and mark the length of the foot from toe and heel against the folded edge as well as the widest point of the foot, taking the measurements from your model. Then draw in the half of the foot in the shape you are planning and cut out the folded halves. It is now ready to be checked for a perfect fit.

Lined footpad. If you want to have a bear which stands by itself or one which has flat soles then you might consider lining the feet with cardboard innersoles. This is very easy to do once you have designed your footpad size. Merely draw another matching footpad and cut off the seam allowance. This will leave you with a template for the innersole. After the leg is sewn and turned, the cardboard innersole is slipped into place against the footpad fabric from the inside and the leg is then stuffed. The stuffing pushes down the innersole and holds it in place. Sometimes extra weighting is added for balance in the legs using steel shot or plastic pellets.

The one-piece straight leg. *Fig. 23A.* Working against the folded edge of your paper, mark in the overall length of your leg from your measurements of the body and arm. Copy the top curve and the joint marker from the arm to ensure equal bulk and the same disc size for all the limbs. Taper the leg in from the thigh down to the ankle, coming in as far for the ankle roughly to the width of the wrist. Decide on the length of the foot and use about half that length for the height of the foot's instep. Curve in at the ankle and come down to a slope at the toe. You have now designed a simple and well-balanced one-piece leg!

As in the one-piece arm the advantage is that you have less sewing and less visible seams, but you also have the same disadvantage; that is, the part of the limb against the fabric fold will be straight. Should you want to have a straight leg but have some shape to the back of the leg, then you will need to design a two-piece leg.

The two-piece straight leg. *Fig. 23B.* Many commercial designs tend to have patterns for two-piece legs (as well as arms) when really a one-piece pattern would do. If the back of the leg is straight from the end of the thigh curve down to the heel then there is no real advantage in making it in two pieces. If you perhaps want to curve out at the back of the thigh and taper in at the ankle but essentially still create a straight leg, then the two-piece pattern win enable you to do that.

The opening is commonly left at the back of the leg, as opposed to the one-piece leg where it has to be at the front.

The V-shaped one-piece straight leg. *Fig. 23C.* This is a less common pattern design, but one you might have come across in commercial kits. The reason for the V-shape in the sole of the foot is to counteract the pulling in at the inner ankle, which sometimes occurs, particularly on larger bears. Of course the other alternative is to clip the inner ankle curve before turning the leg.

This style of leg could also be used on a pattern where you intend the toes to droop a little, in which case you might even accentuate the V-shape.

The two-piece bent leg. *Fig. 23D.* Bent legs are a more contemporary design characteristic for bears, but one which enables the bear to adopt a variety of poses, especially when the stuffing is soft. With bent legs a bear can sit in a chair, hang his legs over the edge of a shelf, cross his legs at the knee or even sit cross-legged.

The opening for such a bent leg pattern would tend to be at A in *Fig. 23D* in order to allow easy access to the joint as well as to the toe for stuffing.

Cross-Checking for a Perfect Fit

Now that you have all your paper pattern pieces it is important to make sure that they are all going to fit together without any problems. We will go through our checklist in the same order as we designed our pieces.

The head. The side head pieces and the head gusset need to fit together smoothly from the tip of the nose down to the back of the neck. Holding the side head piece and the gusset together at the "eye spots" (*Fig. 25A*) you should be able to bend the tip of the nose on the side head piece around until it easily touches the middle of the end of the head gusset (*Fig. 25B*). If the nose on the side head piece cannot reach the middle of the head gusset, the nose on the head gusset can be trimmed back a little and then measured again. Remember that you will have a seam allowance at the tip of the nose on the side head pieces, so allow a little extra for that by ensuring that the nose *easily* reaches the middle of the head gusset's nose (at point B) and not almost reaches it.

It is always better, if possible, to trim the length off the head gusset's nose than off the side pieces. If the head gusset's nose is too short it may be better to cut another (on a folded paper for a symmetrical shape) with a slightly longer nose and try the fit again, rather than cut down the nose on the side pieces and lose the length you may have been aiming for.

Once point A-B in *Fig. 25* fit together nicely you can feel confident that the muzzle on your bear will pin and sew together well. The second check for the head involves the rest of the gusset and its fit down the back of the head.

Hold the "eye spots" together on your side head piece and your gusset piece once again, as in *Fig. 26A*. Now bend the head gusset around until the lower end of it meets the bottom of the neck of the side head piece, at point B. If the gusset cannot reach the end of the neck it is too short and you may have to cut another one with a longer end.

More than likely, however, your gusset will be longer than the neck and can easily be trimmed back to be in alignment with the end of the neck on the side piece. Now you know that the head gusset is long enough to fit the head. While you are holding the gusset curved to the side head piece, also check how the two curves match. Does the rise of the forehead back from point A match on both pieces? Is the widest part of the head gusset at the midway point through the depth of the head? Does it look balanced?

Any minor trimming that is necessary can be done at this stage to make sure that you are happy with the fit of the pieces. Having checked these major points you can now set aside the head.

The ears. Fold the ear in half to check that it is symmetrical and make sure that it has an adequate length to allow a good turning under of the raw edge once it is sewn.

The body. If you are using a four-piece body, take a back and a tummy piece and hold them together so that the side seams match up, as in *Fig. 27* from point A-B. The curve should match perfectly and if it does not it can be trimmed. A matching curve will mean that the side seams will join smoothly. Make sure that the darts are also accurate.

Check the overall length of the two pieces. They should match perfectly also and they should be trimmed if necessary too, otherwise the body will not fit together properly. Also, see if the average thickness of the back and tummy pieces balance each other.

Now flatten the pieces out so that you are looking at a side view of the body and match up the lower darts, as in *Fig. 27C*. If the curve looks like the solid line, then the base of the body will need to be trimmed down to approximately the dotted line. What has happened is that the curves of the bottom and the lower tummy are too heavy and when the darts pull together the result is a dip in the base of the body. In order to achieve a more natural looking curve under the body you will need to trim some of the weight off. It may only apply to one side of the body or to both, but you should finish up with a smooth rounded curve underneath the body from front to back.

Finally, rock the two pieces along the side seam curves until the top darts are pulled together (*Fig. 27D*) and check that the alignment you have aimed for in the neck works and is at the correct angle. It may be horizontal or even tilted forward, but both halves should line up in the same direction.

If you are working with a two-piece body then you only need to check that the darts fit and that the body lines up, using the last two points (as in *Fig. 27C* and *D*). Just pinch them together and see how they look in length, alignment and effect. You may need to trim down the curve under the body a little to improve the effect of the darts and the shape of the finished body.

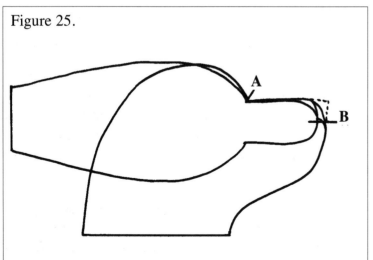

Figure 25.

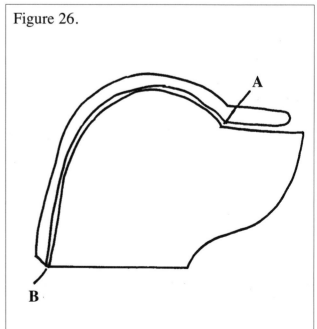

Figure 26.

Make sure that the joint markers are centered between the front and back halves of the body. Ideally they should be just above the inner end of the lower dart and just below the inner end of the top dart. This means that the limbs will cover the ends of the darts and sit nicely at the edge of the shoulders and hips.

The arms. If working with a one-piece arm, fold it in half and make sure that the edges meet all the way around. With two-piece arms, hold the two halves together and check for a perfect match. If for example the inner arm is a little thinner than the outer then sewing it like that will result in it twisting inward. The paw pad should fit snugly all the way around the paw and have either a seam allowance or not, depending on the look you are aiming for. Make sure that the joint marks are centered.

The legs. As with the arms, fold or hold the two halves together and check carefully all the way around the piece for correlation. The footpad can be checked for size by pinching the foot closed where the seam or seams will go and holding the pad against the opening. If the leg is a one-piece pattern you can also place the center of the footpad heel against the heel crease of the leg and fold each side of the foot around the footpad. The sides should easily touch, allowing just enough for the seam.

If the footpad seems slightly big at this stage, don't worry about a final trim until you are actually sewing it in as it might end up being just right. If it appears too small however, do have a larger pattern cut. It is always easy to trim down a piece that is too big, but hard to salvage a piece that is too small.

All together now! *Fig. 28A* and *B*. By placing your pattern pieces together like a paper doll on the table you will be able to get an idea of how the proportions look. It is a good way of also telling you if something is either wrong or just not going to work.

If you have a four-piece body, overlap a tummy and a back piece until the darts almost meet (as in *Fig. 28A*). With a two-piece body you will find that the darts, when sewn, pull in and make the neck area narrower than it appears (*Fig. 28B*). Place the side head piece on the neck but overlap it as you will be losing some of the neck length when you gather in around the neck disc. The head will also appear larger once the head gusset is added to give it three dimensions so do not be concerned if it looks rather small at this stage. If you like you can place the ear on but remember that it will also be smaller, as it will have the edges turned under and it will be curved.

The arms and legs can be placed over the joint spots and you can see what the bear will look like, both standing and seated. When he is seated you can see how the arms will rest and whether they are the right length to give the effect you want. Now you will also be able to see how much room is available between the limbs and ensure that the limbs are not too bulky or perhaps too skinny for the body.

This is by no means a perfect way of visualizing your bear at this stage, but it can really help in identifying any major proportion problems. Such problems should be unlikely at this stage though and your new bear should be looking great - if a bit flat!

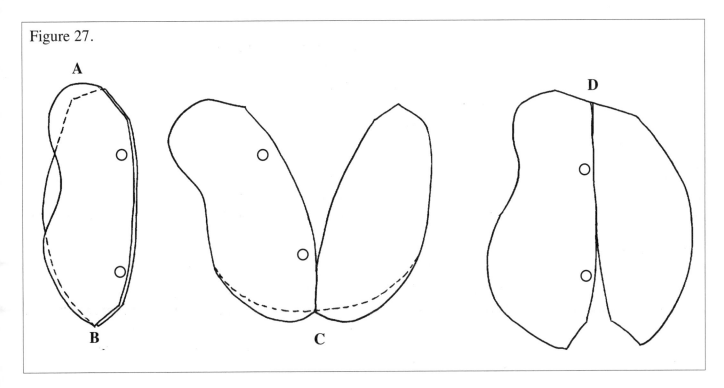

Figure 27.

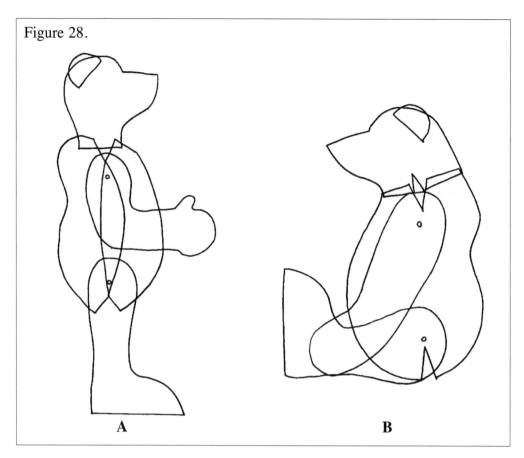

Figure 28.

A   B

Making A Hard Copy

Once you have checked all your pieces and are happy with the look of your paper doll/bear, you can transfer them to a hard-wearing material such as patchwork quilt plastic template or art board for reuse.

Using the patchwork quilt plastic template sheeting is as easy as it is transparent. All you have to do is place your paper pattern pieces underneath it and draw over the edges. It can also be easier to cut out than thick cardboard and the edges do not soften with use, meaning that your plastic pattern templates will have a longer life than those on cardboard will. Even waste plastic such as that cut from the sides of ice cream cartons can be useful and economical for patterns.

You may decide to make all your pattern pieces (that is two side head pieces, four ear pieces, four body pieces etc.) or just have one of each, depending on how you like to work. If you are unsure whether or not your pattern will fit onto a certain piece of fabric, it can save time and avoid frustration if you have every piece on hand. All your pieces can be laid out on the fabric prior to cutting in order to see if they will fit, and you can also play around with the layout like a jigsaw puzzle in order to get the best fit and most economical use of the fabric.

If you have just one of each of the pattern pieces, remember to flip over the pieces that need to be doubled and also remember not to mark your joint holes on all your arm and leg pieces but only once on each side.

Be very careful in copying your patterns to your plastic or cardboard, and make sure you are as accurate as possible in both the marking and the cutting. It is a good idea to go back and cross-check all your pieces again once they are in the plastic or card, in case any small changes might cause problems in the construction of your pattern.

Mark down all relevant details on each pattern piece, such as fur direction and seam openings. Punch in the joint openings with either an awl or a hole punch. Finally, keep all your pattern pieces together. Keep them together in a ziplock-type plastic bag marked with the bear's details such as date of design, height and joint disc size; or by punching a hole in the corner of each piece and attaching them all on a plastic shower curtain ring like keys on a key-ring!

Don't throw out your original paper pattern however, as this should also be kept in a separate ziplock-type bag and labeled. It is good security to always have a duplicate of your pattern kept in a different place in case one gets lost, stolen or damaged.

Pattern Filing and Family Trees

Your working pattern and your original paper pattern, although they may be in different places, should have the same **filing system** for easy access. You might decide to file your patterns according to size, date of design, name or maybe in family groups. Your bears will develop their own family groups as you try the same pattern in different sizes or perhaps with minor variations, such as an inset muzzle or an inset chest in a second color.

You might decide to keep separate **fact sheets** that lists all your patterns ingredients, for example: eye size, disc size, joint size, fur length, etc. This gives you an easy reference guide each time you want to use any of your patterns. If not kept as a separate file, the relevant details can always be kept with each of the patterns.

Taking **photographs** of your work is useful not only for catalogues but also to give you a record of your personal development. If taking photographs for your catalogues, put several bears into each picture to cut down on reproduction costs but do not squeeze in so many bears that the details are lost in the crowd. A good photograph of your bear is one without distracting background colors and details and which is clear and close up, but where you see the whole bear. Having the bear looking at the camera also helps to create that alive look.

As you start designing and making bears, it is important to keep track of not only what you are doing but of where it all came from. You may find that your patterns started from an amalgamation of a commercial pattern, with your own variations and added ideas. These first couple of bears can be the ancestors of a whole dynasty of bears.

Keeping several **notebooks** can be a good way of organizing things. One should be an Ideas Book that is always kept at hand for jotting down ideas for designs, accessories and other future projects. Pictures from magazines, and photos or sketches from the zoo can all be great additions to your Ideas Book. Another notebook could be your Design Index, where you list in chronological order the date and name of the design along with details of the pattern's background and lineage.

It can be helpful to use some sort of a coding system in the names you give the bears. This means that, while you may have forgotten that one bear is sort of related to the other, the name will remind you of its origins. Naming each bear you make, especially if you give a different name to every bear even if they are from the same pattern, can be confusing in the long run. It can also be exhausting to keep coming up with new names all the time.

It is much easier to give each pattern a name instead, and merely number the bears from that pattern so for example, you might be working on Jackson 12. It can also be helpful to make a note (perhaps in your Design Index) of the number of the last bear you made of each particular pattern as you will undoubtedly have several patterns going at once. That way you will know where you are up to with each pattern. If you have already decided on an edition size he could then be Jackson 12/15 or maybe Jackson 12/20. Of course he may be only a one-of-a-kind in which case he would be Jackson 1/1. Don't be overly ambitious in your edition size, even if you make a pattern which you think is great. By the time you get down to making Jackson 75/100 it is a sure thing that you will never want to see that pattern again and more than likely you will be making better patterns than that anyway!

Apart from the details you keep in your Design Index, your bears' names can tell you a lot about their family tree with just a little organization. Say that you design a 14in (36cm) bear called Montgomery, and reduce it down to a 7in (18cm) size also. The smaller version could be called either Little Montgomery or just Monty. You might go on to change the pattern but as Montgomery was the ancestor, if you call the new bear something beginning with the same first few letters, like Morris, then it will help remind you where he came from.

You might decide a whole family of bears will have the same letter to begin their names, or they may have a link in that they are all named after historical figures, or trees or even your own family members!

Think of your bears and their family trees right from the start, as a little planning will make a lot of sense. The orderly progression of your work as the genealogical lines unfold will not only show the evolution of your bears but also provide a fascinating personal history in years to come.

Styles and Themes

This is the dream factory stuff, and where your Idea Books come in handy. It is the creative urge that keeps us wanting to do more but we need inspiration, and that can come from within or without. If you are a vivid dreamer then you might like to keep your Ideas Book next to the bed and write down those ideas before they fade. If you don't think that your imagination is that active, then keep an eye out for ideas all around you.

Apart from specific ideas for design aspects in your patterns, you might think about styles and themes for your work. It is important to feel as though you are continually moving forward, and not in just your creative endeavors. Stagnation may be the death of creativity but life is also about continually acquiring knowledge and experience and hopefully being able to put them both to good use.

Once you have become comfortable with a particular look or technique in your bear making, perhaps it is time to push yourself out of that comfort zone and try something new. Often taking up a challenge, such as agreeing to do a charity auction piece, can provide the impetus you might need to get yourself out of a creative rut.

Think about new themes for whole lines of bears. There are many influences which can affect our senses and inspire us, such as cinema, theatre, art, music, history, nature or travel.

Characters from a film, period costumes in a play, the colors or themes of an artist, the gods of ancient Egypt, a family of favorite flowers, or architectural detail from a beloved cathedral are possible inspirations. There is no limit as to what can affect us emotionally and what we can creatively put to use.

As some examples, if you want to make a series of dressed bears and are an opera buff, what about making all the characters from your favorite opera? You might design the costumes yourself or even choose to research them in the library and accurately recreate the costumes used in a certain production. Perhaps you were impressed with the costumes in a period film you saw and want to create historical costumes of a certain era. Rent the video to sketch and note down details of the costumes you like. An amazing amount of detail can be picked up from the video, especially when you can stop and rewind.

A walk through your nearest botanic gardens can inspire whole lineages of bears, not merely through the wonderful Latin names but also through the exotic flowers and berries of plants from all over the world. Wandering around the art gallery can also be a wonderful source of inspiration. If you cannot find anything in the artworks themselves to give you ideas, what about the names alone? Hepworth, Moore, Calder, Mondrian, Olsen, Henry, Georgia, Frida, Pablo - there are a thousand great bear's names in any art gallery.

BEAR CONSTRUCTION

The good news is that making teddy bears does not require a huge amount of tools and hardware. Most bear makers can fit all their tools (apart from the sewing machine) into a portable fishing tackle box. If you stitch by hand, you can be even more compact and convert a makeup or toiletries bag into a special traveling tool kit for making bears on planes, trains and automobiles.

Essential Tools

The sewing machine. Virtually any type of sewing machine can be used in the making of teddy bears, from an antique foot-operated treadle machine to the latest computer-driven sewing machine. It all depends on how you like to sew and what you feel comfortable with. You might find that when using a sewing machine a couple of items will help you, especially when tackling those tricky shapes. The narrowest foot you can find will enable you to see what you are doing and gauge the correct seam allowance, and a knee-lift mechanism will virtually give you an extra hand when negotiating those tight curves and working on small pieces.

When using a sewing machine the main thing to practice on is your accuracy rather than your speed. The speed will come when you are confident, but no one except yourself will know how fast or slow you are on the machine. It is the accuracy of your sewing (or lack thereof!) that will be a lasting testament to your work, so take your time.

The tool box. Hardware and fishing tackle shops have a good variety of portable boxes that make excellent bear making tool boxes. They are usually in a durable plastic with a carry handle and they open out to give easy access to several drawers and lots of containers.

Also to be found in hardware stores are flat plastic stackable boxes with lots of small compartments, excellent for tiny things like eyes, charms, miniature joints, beads and buttons.

Needles and pins. Even if you sew by machine you will need a range of hand sewing needles, particularly for closing the seams. **Sharps** with large eyes or **darners** are good as you will usually be using a strong, fairly heavy thread to close. If you stitch by hand then the size of the needle will depend on what you are used to working with. Those people with embroidery backgrounds might be used to working with much smaller needles and may find darners a bit cumbersome to use. The needle size will also be governed to an extent by the thickness of the thread you use, as the eye will have to take the thread.

The other kind of needles you will need are a range of **doll needles**, or long needles for sewing in the eyes. These range from 3in (8cm) up to 12in (31cm). The 3in (8cm) size is good for embroidering noses and claws. While the ordinary sewing needles can be kept in a needle case, the large doll needles should be handled carefully as they could be lethal weapons! (They also have been confiscated from airline flights on occasion.) Try keeping them stuck in a cork.

If you are using leather or suede for paw pads and hand stitching them in you will need to use **leather needles**. These are very sharp needles with a triangular point, which slices through the thick leather. They come in many sizes but the larger ones may make too large a hole, so try to use the smaller or glover's needles, available from leathercraft suppliers.

The best pins to use are the **glass headed** or **berry pins**, and **quilting** pins have the advantage of being nice and long too. The colored heads make the pins harder to lose in fur, particularly when pinning in the ears. If you are working on a large bear you might find the pins do not hold the ears on satisfactorily. In that case, try using the heavier **wig pins** which have a T-shaped end. They are harder to get in but will not bounce back out so readily.

For areas which need to be pinned but perhaps have delicate edges which might fray or retain the hole marks (for example antique fabrics or thin suede), try using tiny **alligator clips**, available from automotive shops.

Thimbles. Using thimbles is a bit of an acquired art, but one which could save you scarred fingertips. Callused fingers are an inevitable part of long term bear making, but that is no reason not to try and protect your hands. Bear making involves a lot of fine handwork and it can be hard work getting stubborn needles through tightly stuffed portions of the body. Try using a standard

metal thimble on the finger, which is getting the most wear. If you tend to avoid using the thimble rather than using it to push with, try some other type of finger protector, which may feel more natural.

You can make yourself a **leather fingerstall** and even line it with a small piece of metal to protect your fingertip when pushing needles. A **leather finger sleeve** can also protect against cut fingers when pulling in and knotting the eye threads. Even a **fabric Band-Aid** can help give extra protection and make those fingers last a little longer.

Scissors and knives. There is a lot of cutting involved in bear making, from the first snip into your piece of fabric to the final trimming of the bear's features. Different scissors will suit each job, and consequently you will tend to have quite a few pairs, including your favorite and the paper cutting pair. Keep your scissors sharp for a longer life, either by regularly sharpening them yourself or having them done professionally.

There are many brands of scissors on the market, but whether you are looking for large shears or small pointed trimming scissors, look for good comfortable grips and quality steel blades. Doing a lot of cutting with scissors can be very hard on the thumb joints, and you might think of trying (if you are not already using them) some of the new scissors which are spring-loaded and do not have thumb rings. The **Fiskars** brand is excellent and has both large shears and small trimming scissors in its spring-loaded range, as well as a good scissors sharpener.

Another way of saving your thumb joints is to use cutting blades for cutting out your pattern pieces, and these are available from handicraft shops.

Awls and punches. You will need to punch holes in both your fabric for the joints and in the pattern pieces to mark the joint holes, as well as making holes for the eyes. In fact, anywhere you wish to make a hole, an awl or something with a sharp point should be used in preference to cutting a hole with scissors. A cut hole may fray but a pierced hole tends to be less damaging to the fabric, as it pushes apart the weave rather than cuts it.

Marking pens. A good **indelible felt marking pen** with a fine tip is good for marking out your fabric, sometimes **ballpoint pens** can work just as well. **Fading fabric markers** can be good, but you may find that the temperature affects their performance and in hot climates they may fade before you can even cut out your pieces! A good color range of indelible felt marking pens is now available, and these are great for adding subtle "painted" details to your bear.

Joint fasteners. The type of fastening tool you will need will depend on what type of jointing system you use. If you use cotter or split pins, discs and washers you will need either a pair of needle-nosed pliers or preferably a **cotter key**. These are readily available from bear making suppliers (see Suppliers Index). This is basically a small screwdriver, which has been given a split down the end and it works in the same way as the key on a tin of sardines. You slot one end of the cotter pin into the cotter key at a time and roll it down until it is snug against the disc.

If you are using pop-rivets for the joints then you will need a **pop-rivet gun**, available at hardware shops, along with your supply of rivets. You use them in conjunction with the normal washers and discs.

For locknut and bolt joints you need to hold the end of the bolt in order to fasten on the nut, so you need two tools. If you are using a slot-ended bolt then you will need a screwdriver to hold the bolt and a **nut driver** or nut spinner to tighten the nut. A nut driver is an hexagonal cup on a screwdriver handle that fits over the nut or hex bolt end to hold it still. (Nut drivers come in a wide range of sizes to fit your joints.) You might find that a screwdriver can slip and possibly strip the head of a slot-ended bolt, and possibly a Phillips bolt with a Phillips screwdriver might give better leverage. Better still, using hexagonal head nuts and bolts gives good non-slip ends for your jointing tools.

A pair of nut drivers will do the job of fastening locknuts, but you might like to try a nut driver to hold the bolt and a **ratchet spanner** or **wrench** to turn on the nuts with. This ratchet spanner (wrench) is compact and much more convenient than an ordinary wrench, as little movement is needed to tighten or loosen the nut. They have an "on" and "off" side (or on/off lever) and they come in various sizes with a different size on each end.

Glues and waxes. There are a few different types of glues, which are handy to have. A spray adhesive is good for gluing on a thin cotton backing to stretchy or fragile fabrics in order to strengthen them.

Fray-chek or **Fraystopper** can be used to strengthen the edges of fabric to stop it from fraying. If you find the edges are too stiff with these glues, try a water-based woodworking or **craft glue** and dilute it 50% with water. The resulting glue will be the consistency of milk and will dry to an invisible and rubbery finish.

Superglue is also very handy for fusing nuts onto bolts and creating locknuts (see Jointing Systems section), especially for the neck bolt. Alternatively, other threadlockers such as Loctite can be used.

A rubbery **contact adhesive** is also convenient for gluing on nose templates and appliquéd paw pad details prior to stitching. A **hot glue gun** can be great for fixing on details to accessories, such as small silk flowers onto straw hats or when making flower and berry garlands.

Beeswax is good for a variety of uses. It can be used to stiffen sewing threads prior to use, and is great when melted and used to polish stitched noses (see Noses section).

Stuffing tools. You will need different sizes of stuffing tools, depending on what size bear you are stuffing and what part of him you are working on. Simple straight wooden sticks are frequently used, from bamboo cooking **skewers** with the points rounded off for little bears to **chopsticks** and the handles of **wooden spoons**.

Wooden **T-shaped stuffing sticks** are available from bear making suppliers and come in different sizes, as well as with different tips from pointed to chisel shaped to blunt. There are also **metal stuffing tools** that have a grip handle and a forked tip, and these can prove very useful for holding the stuffing as it goes in, particularly when using excelsior.

Other metal stuffing tools that hold the stuffing are **forceps** and **tweezers** (available from pharmacies or medical supply outlets), especially useful for small bears or difficult areas. **Medical clamps** with the locking mechanism filed off can also be used.

You will find that you have your favorite stuffing tools but try to have a variety of different types, not only to cover different situations, but also to give your hands different work and avoid strain.

Wire Brush. These are the fine wire brushes that can be bought from pet shops (made for cats) and they are invaluable for pulling out fur caught in seams, as well as for grooming and trimming. There are also smaller finger versions available through bear suppliers. Be careful when using them near felt paw pads as they can fluff the surface of the felt, and they may also scratch boot button eyes. String mohair should not be brushed unless you want a fluffier look to the fur.

Brushes and airbrushes. If you want to have painted details on your bears, you can do this in a number of different ways. Permanent **fabric dyes** can be applied with small cosmetic **sponges**. **Waterproof inks** can be used with **paintbrushes**. Indelible brush-tipped marker pens can be used, or at the other end of the scale you can use an **airbrush**. If you want to try an airbrush it can be an expensive outlay, but look for one with a fine spray and try an internal mix, dual action tool. For a similar effect at a cheaper price, you might try using an **atomizer** (available from a pharmacy or chemist) loaded with colored inks.

Just remember that whatever you use, it needs to be waterproof or indelible so that it will not smudge or run over time, or if it should get damp.

Extra equipment. It could be a good idea to have an **air cleaner**, especially if you are prone to asthmatic conditions. This is a small plug-in machine that actually draws in the dust and other minute particles out of the air.

Face masks can also be very useful particularly when stuffing or cutting fur. There are many available, from simple paper disposable ones to expensive dual action filter masks that look like gas masks. Some may be hard to breathe through for extended peri-ods however, or hot to work in, so look around till you find something that suits you.

A **magnifying glass** is also a good idea for small work and to avoid eye strain. You can get a table-mounted version or even a type that stands on the floor and has a lighted rim.

Audio books from the library are a great way of keeping up with your reading as you work. Music can be soothing, but after a while you may feel that you need more of a mental stimulation while you sew. With an audio book you can do two things at once, read and sew, and it feels as though you are making good use of your time. If your local library does not stock any audio books, or perhaps has a poor selection, you can join book clubs or even get together with friends and share some purchased ones around.

Jointing Systems

Disc and string joints. Fig 29A. Possibly the earliest type of jointing for teddy bears, disc and string joints were used by Steiff for a short period around 1903 to 1904. This consisted of twine thread jointing through heavy cardboard discs. While it did enable the bear's limbs and head to move it was found to be too loose and the bear tended to flop rather than hold its pose. (For a short while at the end of 1904 Steiff tried using a patented system of attaching the cardboard joints with double wires which were twisted together in the center of the body.)

Rod system. Steiff's "improved" system in 1905 consisted of a metal rod connecting the arms and head, and one connecting the legs, as in *Fig. 29B*. In each limb there is a disc and metal pin, allowing the limb to rotate. The head also swiveled on its rod. While this type of jointing system worked, it added a lot of weight to the bear and also tended to become quite loose. It was quickly superseded by the disc and "nail" joint system.

Disc and "nail" joints. From 1905 onwards, Steiff has used a

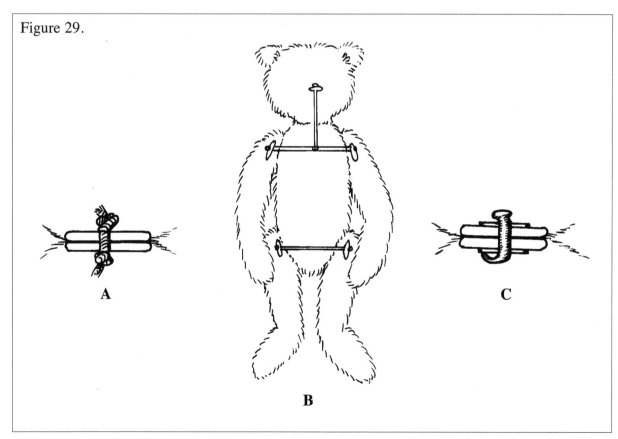

Figure 29.

A

B

C

strong reliable system of jointing for their bears and many other animal toys. The thick cardboard discs and metal washers from the string system were retained but the pinning mechanism was changed to a metal pin, rather like a nail which was bent over at the end to secure it, as in *Fig. 29C*. This is the most common jointing mechanism for bears made by Steiff, and many other manufacturers today.

Snap Joints. These were another innovation of Steiff's in 1908, using Carl Pfenning's 1895 invention of the snap-fastener for mens' trousers. Removable joints were designed for "Roly Poly" figures to enable them to also be played with as a ball and teddy bears were also given these "snap-a-part" limbs. This novelty line lasted for a few years.

Ball-joints. Another novel approach by Steiff was to create a neck mechanism with a universal movement, as in *Fig. 30A*. This was patented in 1908 and was used in their poodle, pig, cat, opossum and polar bear designs. Covered by fabric on the neck there was a neck socket holding a rod connected to a ball fixed in the head and the resulting movement was very realistic.

Plastic "popjoints". Often called "doll" joints, these are simple plastic pieces, one shaped like a mushroom and the other a ring which grips around the ribbed stalk of the mushroom. Frequently used for cheaper mass-produced soft toys today, these joints are also readily available in craft shops. There can be several problems with this style of joint, however. The head of the joint (mushroom) is often not large enough and there is no allowance made for adding a disc, resulting in a "puffed sleeve" look to the shoulder and thigh. When the fastening ring is mapped on to the joint shaft it cannot be adjusted, which often leaves the limb too loose.

While suitable for some soft toys and crafts, this type of jointing system is not really adequate for the artist made bear, where something more adaptable and adjustable is required.

Cotter pin or split pin joints. Fig. 30B. As in Steiff's modern jointing system discs and metal washers are used, but instead of the single bent-over metal pin a split pin is used and the ends are rolled down and away from each other. The discs may be heavy cardboard, plywood, craftboard or some other composite material. This type of joint is commonly used as it is easy to work with. The main thing to remember with it is to use as heavy a pin as possible for the size of the bear you are making. This will ensure durability and prevent loosening of the joint over time.

The cotter pin or split pin joint is often used in conjunction with locknut joints in one bear, where the locknuts are used on the limbs and the cotter pin on the head. (See Jointing section.)

Pop rivet joints. This jointing system is sometimes used in manufacturing teddy bears and soft toys, as it can be very quick. A rivet gun (professional ones may use compressed air) fires nail-like rivets and flattens them out on the ends producing a very strong fastening. Adjustments cannot be made afterwards, however, so it is necessary to get it right first time. Practicing on cheaper materials can be a good idea, and you might find that you need a removable layer between the discs in order to get adequate movement of the joint. Try using a sheet of plastic with a slit cut into half of it that you can slide out of the joint after riveting it.

Locknut joints. Fig. 30C. Like the cotter pin or "nail" joints this system also uses discs and metal washers, but as a fastener it uses

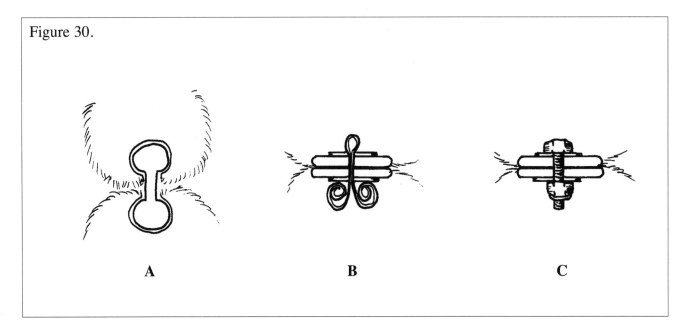

Figure 30.

A   B   C

bolts and locknuts. Locknuts are nuts which have a ring of nylon inside the head. When fastened onto the bolt the nylon ring of the nut jams onto the thread of the bolt. The locknut is tightened by holding the head of the bolt still and forcing the nut down the bolt. In order to do this you need two tools, one to hold the head of the bolt (often a nut driver if you are using an hex head bolt) and one to fasten on the nut (either a ratchet spanner/wrench or another nut driver.)

The advantage of the locknut is that it can be finely adjusted and, once it is fastened to your satisfaction, the nylon insert ensures that it will never loosen. The galvanized steel of the nuts and bolts adds a nice weight to the bear and will never rust.

Loc-Line armature. In recent years there have been some new inventions for achieving more lifelike movement in artist made teddy bears, and these innovations are now flowing on to mass production as well. Loc-Line is a modular system consisting of interlocking plastic segments which pop together with the aid of special pliers. When put together into sections, Loc-Line produces a flexible internal structure which can give the bear a variety of poses. It can be used with connecting X- and Y-shaped fittings to produce a full "skeleton" for the bear, or sections can be used in conjunction with swivel disc joints. If you find that cotter pins are not strong enough to hold the joints, then use the nut and bolt system.

Pad well with strip wadding around the armature before inserting it into the limbs and stitch it lightly to hold it in place. Stuff softly to allow limb movement without ripping the seams. A possible disadvantage in using Loc-Line is that there is a popping or creaking noise as the limb is moved, but it is a great invention, especially for larger bears. Using Teflon Dry Film Spray on the connectors before assembling Loc-Line can help minimize noise during movement.

Flexlimb. Another type of armature inside the bear which allows a greater degree of movement, but one which is noiseless, is Flexlimb. This is essentially plastic coated electrical wire threaded through a cylinder of foam with a metal ring at one end. It is available in different lengths and thicknesses, depending on the size of the bear you are working on. The ring end fits onto either a cotter pin or tap bolt and the other end is cut to size and the wire bent over to secure the foam. As with Loc-Line, stuff softly to allow limb movement and slightly larger openings may need to be left to allow the insertion of the Flexlimb or Loc-Line.

Mechanical joints. Possibly the earliest of the novelty joint mechanisms was the **Somersault** mechanism, first patented by the Paris based toy company of Ernest Descamp in 1908, but similar styles were also used by Strunz, Steiff and Bing. The bear's arms acted as the key and were turned to wind it up. When released the bear flipped over and over doing forward somersaults. (In 1909 Steiff had somersaulting bears, monkeys, elephants, clowns and Eskimo dolls on the market, while Strunz had a whole series of somersaulting toys called Barnum's Animals.)

Other **clockwork** mechanisms using keys were placed in teddy bears and toys from quite early on and included walking, skating and sweeping bears and heads that moved from side to side. The Bing company was known for its clockwork toys, as was Schuco.

The toy company Shreyer & Co. (Schuco) of Nuremberg was the first to register and use the **Yes/No** mechanism in 1921, with Steiff and America following with similar designs in 1931 and 1932. This mechanism is basically a rod through the length of the body from the head to the tail and head movement is controlled by using the tail as a lever.

The **Swivel/Tilt** neck mechanism is a more recent invention, by American bear artist Barbara Wiltrout. It enables a bear to move its head on a universal joint, using an aluminum spring-loaded curved disc (for the head) that sits in a cup (for the neck).

Mechanisms

Apart from the mechanical jointing systems mentioned above, there are other mechanisms which can be placed inside teddy bears' bodies in order to give them voices or to make music. The earliest of these was the **press squeaker** or squeeze-box, often placed in the side or the tummy. The **tilt growler** followed, and there was also a **pull string growler** that was often used in wheeled animals. Although the style and materials may have changed from the early day of manufacture, squeakers and growlers are still readily available.

Similarly, **music boxes** have been used in bears for many years. Music boxes can have fixed keys, detachable keys or pull cords. The original Swiss mechanisms have now been replaced by music boxes that come from Japan.

If using any type of internal mechanism in your bear, ensure that the body will be big enough for it . Growlers and music boxes are not suitable for bears under about twelve inches high.Also, be certain that the opening in the back of the body will be large enough to accommodate the mechanism. There should be sufficient stuffing all around the mechanism so that it cannot be felt from the outside. Pellet stuffing in the body is not ideal in such a bear as it can often result in a music box or growler shifting. If you want a pellet filled body you might try putting the growler in the head!

If you are using a growler, cover the perforated end with a fine fabric to prevent stuffing from "suffocating" the mechanism. With music boxes, make sure that you have an adequate length of shaft protruding so that the key does not jam up with fur.

Smaller modern flat or concertina **plastic squealers** and tiny **music "buttons"** are a convenient size for using in little bears. Even **bells** can be used inside bears' ears, paws or tummies.

FABRICS

Mohair pile fabric (shorn from the angora goat and woven into a cotton backing) has always been the traditional teddy bear fabric, and it was used for both the first American Ideal bears as well as the German Steiffs. At the time that the teddy bear came into being mohair fabric was not uncommon and had many uses, from upholstery to coat fabrics. Perfect for the teddy bear, mohair was soft yet hard-wearing and had the look of a real fur.

Never a cheap fabric to make, these days mohair is produced by only a handful of factories and almost solely for the teddy bear trade. Although the number of producers of mohair pile fabric may be small the variety available today is huge. We are very fortunate to have a much greater diversity of color, length, thickness and style than ever before, with new types appearing every year.

From the initial brown, gold and white mohair of the first bears, we now have over 900 different mohair fabrics to choose from, ranging from 3/16in (.45cm) to 3in (8cm) long. Apart from straight colors there is a large range of tipped mohair incorporating two colors, as well as color-blend that has darker hairs interspersed into the pile. There are standard thicknesses, extra dense, sparse and extra sparse. There are curly, wavy, distressed and feathered or V-cut finishes to the pile. Some types of mohair has been deliberately aged to have less of a sheen, while others may have a backing of a different color to the pile. Mohair is also available in its undyed and uncombed state as "string" mohair. Some mohair fabrics have a lot of sizing or stiffening in the backing, while others have very little and this can affect fraying and stretching as well as the ease with which it is handled. You can even boil your piece of mohair before using it in order to shrink it and tighten the weave to help prevent fraying.

With all these types of mohair fabric available to the bear maker today, the only question is where to start? Of course, if you can find nothing to suit you, you can always custom dye your mohair, as well as straighten, distress or antique the pile and the color. (One way of making the mohair look more faded or discolored is to spray on brown fabric dye in patches with a spray bottle. If you are hand-dyeing small quantities of mohair you can speed up the process by using the microwave.) Apart from pure mohair there are also mohair blend fabrics on the market and you might like to try mohair with alpaca, wool silk or cotton for a different feel.

There are two distinct groups of mohair fabric, the English and the German. There may not be much difference in the price, but in general you will find that you can distinguish between the two by looking at the backing. The backing in the English mohair tends to have a slightly coarser weave than the German. In some cases this coarser weave may also mean that it is a little looser, so check that it does not stretch or distort. Sizing in the backing can always counteract this, of course. Your decision to use one type of mohair over the other may be based on proportion, too. The backing is most apparent around the muzzle where the fur is trimmed back, and while a coarser backing works well on a larger bear perhaps a finer backing is preferable on a smaller bear.

Often you will find that your choice of fabric will dictate what type of bear you make. For example, a sparse mohair would suit an old-looking, worn type of bear while a dense tipped mohair may be better suited to a more realistic wild bear. It can be very exciting to come across an appealing new color or a type of fur you have not used before, as it really sparks the imagination and you can visualize what sort of bear should be made out of that fabric.

This is the same creative force that enables a sculptor to "see" the figure or shape inside a piece of stone or wood. For the Native American fetish carvers of New Mexico it means even more. The appropriateness of the material to the subject is a starting point, but they believe that their smaller sculpted animal figures also have the soul or breath of that animal inside it. It is also an interesting coincidence that among most Native American groups the bear is especially popular and is known for its healing associations.

Synthetic materials were first invented in the 1920s and took over in teddy bear making after World War II. These days it is usually only the collector's bears which are still made in mohair. There are now some excellent synthetic plush matreials available, however, especially those which are as thick and luxurious as sable and have lifelike guard hairs.

The top quality synthetics can be almost as expensive as mohair, but have quite a different feel and look. The finer man-made fibers give a softer fur than mohair and often one that is much denser. If using synthetic fur, try to ensure that it has a tightly woven backing rather than a knitted one. Knit-back synthetics may be cheaper but will stretch and distort. If you have some knit-back synthetic fabric you can make it less stretchy by lining it before use. Using spray adhesive, coat the back of the synthetic and glue on a layer of thin cotton fabric or some other non-stretch material.

Rayon is made up to produce a different type of synthetic plush fabric, and comes in curly, straight, matted, silky, distressed and a flat pile. The length tends to be rather short so rayon is suitable for small bears.

Real fur. It is now not socially or politically correct to wear animal furs, but there are a lot of old fur coats around that can be usefully recycled into great teddy bears. If you do not have any fur coats or wraps lurking at the back of your closet you might find some wonderful furs at your local thrift shops for very little money.

The first thing that you need to ensure is that the fur still has a good leather backing. After taking off the satin lining of the coat or wrap have a look at the condition of the skin. If it is old the leather may have deteriorated into a fragile parchment. You will also see the seams of the skins and if the original animals were small (for example marmot, squirrel or mink), the skins will be very narrow.

If the leather has lost its flexibility it may tear like a sheet of perforated paper when you sew it. In order to protect it, line it by gluing on a fabric backing before you use it. A blade can be very handy for cutting out your pieces, and double-stitching all your seams can also be a good idea to prevent the seams from splitting.

When trimming the fur on the face of the finished bear, be very delicate in your technique. As real fur is often very dense, every little snip mark can show unless you are careful. You might experiment with electric clippers or even a lint-ball shaver.

Material fabrics. For dressed bears, or even as accessories for undressed bears, material fabrics of all kinds can be used. There are some wonderful fabrics with small prints to be found at patchwork supply shops, and many people enjoy hunting out rare and vintage fabrics at flea markets or antique shows. Modern fabrics, ribbons and laces can easily be "antiqued" by dyeing them in tea or coffee. Soft silk ribbons take dyes or even inks well and dipping them into a series of different colors can produce some beautiful watercolor effects.

Laying out your pattern.

The nap of the fur will determine how you lay out your pattern. If you are using a short pile fabric, or one that is very dense, you may not notice a discernible nap or direction to the fur as it may be standing up straight from the backing. In this case you can lay out the pattern pieces as economically as possible by squeezing them in like a jigsaw puzzle, bearing in mind the direction of the grain. If you are using real fur you will find the nap easily and there should be no stretching in the leather backing to worry about.

The grain of the fabric is made up of the horizontal weft and vertical warp threads in the backing. If you pull on the fabric horizontally, vertically and diagonally you will find where its particular stretchiness lies. In most mohair fabrics, as it is tightly woven, there may only be stretch in the diagonal.

When you find the nap on your fabric piece it is useful to mark a little arrow in the corresponding direction on the back. Laying out your pattern pieces is then a simple process of matching up the arrows on each piece with the arrow on the fabric.

If you find that the direction of the fur runs diagonally across the piece of fabric, then you have to make a decision. Do you mark out your pieces following the nap or following the grain of the backing? This really depends on the size of the bear and the tightness of the grain in the backing weave. If the bear is small it will put less pressure on the fabric when stuffed, and if the weave is tight then the fabric will distort less. As a general rule, do always try to avoid masking out on the diagonal, particularly with the head pieces.

Check the stretchiness of your fabric on the diagonal and think about the head, which is the most firmly stuffed part of your bear. If the rest of the bear is going to be softly stuffed then it may not distort, but the head is likely to. If you choose not to cut out your fabric on the diagonal but to follow the grain, the fur will not be going in the direction you want.

Dampening the offending piece of fabric with a spray bottle of water can solve this dilemma. When the pile is wet brush it into the correct direction and iron it dry. Brush again to check if the new direction has held. If it is particularly stubborn (as, for example, with some curly mohair) you might try also combing clear hair gel through the damp fur and setting it with a hair dryer. Brush out the stiffness when it is dry.

When laying out your pattern pieces, try to be as economical as possible. Leave the ears till last rather than make room for them as you will always find little spaces for them around your other pieces. Sometimes the nap can change directions several times in any given piece of fabric, so keep checking as you lay out your pieces. Make sure that the fur for the muzzles of the side head pieces is symmetrical especially if working with distressed or curly mohair.

Marking out. Once you are happy with the layout of your pattern pieces they can be marked out. This is best done with a fairly fine pointed pen, as a thick one will allow too much margin for error in cutting out. With a thin line to follow when you cut out you are forced to be more precise.

Your marking pens should be indelible or waterproof as if you are cutting to the outside of the marked lines the ink will be on the body parts and may smudge or run when you fray-check the edges or if you use painted or airbrushed detailing. If you always cut inside the marked lines and therefore remove your ink from the pieces, it can still be a good idea to use waterproof pens as accidents (such as spilling that cup of coffee over your fabric before you have cut it out) have been known to happen!

Cutting out. This is best done with small, sharp, pointed scissors rather than large dressmaking shears. The reason is that we want to ensure that we cut only the backing fabric and not the fur pile.

Larger scissors tend to chop into the fur, where with smaller scissors you are forced to go more slowly and the smaller snips you make are less likely to cut the edges off the fur. Some people use cutting blades for this, but they take a bit of practice to get used to and the fabric needs to be held taut.

In order to avoid a double edge of fur at your seam edges after you have sewn and turned your pieces, you may choose to trim back the edges as you cut the pieces out. By cutting off the fur in as far as the seam allowance, but no deeper than that, you will also make the pieces easier to sew and stop fur from catching in the seam as you sew it. You can just trim along the muzzle edges, as in the striped areas of *Fig. 31*, or you may decide to trim around the edge of every piece. If you are using a dense or a tipped mohair, then trimming around every edge before you sew can give you a more seamless finish.

Scraps. Any scraps that are left over are useful if they are ear size or larger. You might find it handy to keep scrap bags in sorted colors for the time when you are a bit short of a particular style or color. Sometimes there will be enough left over to make another smaller bear, and if the pile is a bit long it can always be sheared down to an appropriate length.

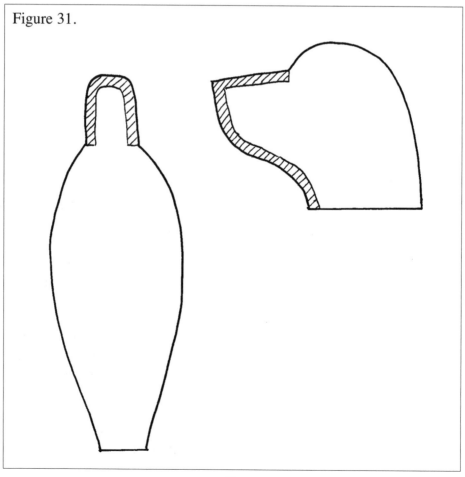

Figure 31.

THREADS

Sewing threads will vary, depending on whether you are machine sewing or hand sewing. Often ordinary machine thread is used for machine work but you might try using a slightly heavier thread for extra strength in your seams.

If you are hand sewing, a good thread to use is the strong **top-stitch** or **buttonhole thread**, usually available in smaller spools (100 to 500 yards or meters) at fabric shops. For large and more economical spools (of 4000 yards or more), **upholstery thread** can be obtained from a wholesale sewing supplier.

Upholstery thread is great for closing seams, but sometimes **artificial sinew** or **dental floss** is used. These two threads may be better used for pulling in eyes and for needle-sculpting. Artificial sinew can be found at leathercraft suppliers and dental floss from pharmacy suppliers, but the sinew is more economical. Each length of the sinew can be split into four almost unbreakable strands and its stickiness helps to hold eyes in place as they are knotted.

Pearl cotton comes in a wide variety of thicknesses and colors and its sheen makes it well suited for embroidering bears' noses. DMC (made in France) is one of the largest manufacturers of sewing and embroidery threads and their pearl cottons are used in bear making around the world. The thickest of the DMC pearl cottons is #3 and this is good for large bears, #5 suits medium bears and #8, 10 and 12 are great for progressively smaller bears.

Other threads that can be used for embroidering noses include **waxed linen** or **carpet threads**. Virtually any strong thread of a suitable thickness with a good sheen and which does not "pill" or untwist can be used for noses.

PINNING

The type of pins or clips that you can use in bear making has already been covered in the Essential Tools section. Unless you are making miniature bears where the pieces are really tiny, pinning is important before the pieces are sewn. This is because any fabric that has a pile or nap tends to travel when placed against itself. If it is not held with pins or clips by the time you have sewn to the end of the seam the edges will not match up.

Match up your pieces carefully as you pin, securing the beginning and end of each seam to ensure a perfect fit. It is a good idea to tuck the ends of the pins into the fabric, as in *Fig. 32*, to prevent the sewing thread catching in them The pins can also be used to push the fur inside the two pieces as you pin them together. They can be removed after the edges have been either hand tacked or as they are sewn by machine.

When pinning the head, first pin the two side pieces together from the point of the muzzle down to the front edge of the neck, as in *Fig. 33A*. This seam will be sewn first and then the head gusset can be pinned in and sewn, as in *Fig. 33B*. After the muzzle of the head gusset is sewn in the rest of the gusset can be pinned (match the neck ends first and ease in around the curve of the head) down each side at a time. This method will ensure that the head gusset is set in squarely and will help eliminate any twisting or distortion of the muzzle.

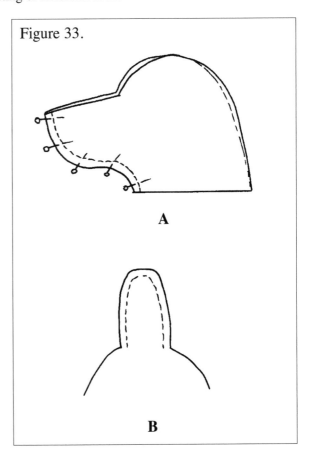

Figure 33.

A

B

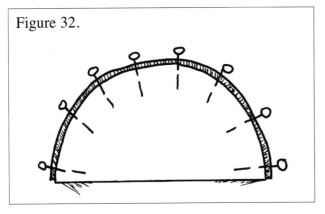

Figure 32.

51

SEWING

A good **seam allowance** is important when sewing. If the seam is sewn too close to the edge there is a fair chance that it will rip apart when the bear is stuffed and that seam is under pressure. A 1/4" allowance is a guide for most bears, but of course the allowance will get slightly smaller with smaller bears.

You will find sewing is easier if you sew with the direction of the fur rather than against it. The fur will be less likely to jam in the seam or to pop back out and get in the way of your sewing.

If **machine sewing** stitch backwards and forwards a few times at the beginning and end of each seam to help anchor the stitches and to prevent unraveling. Adjust your tension so that the seams are firm enough to hold when the piece is stuffed without ripping (too tight) or stretching to show the stitches (too loose).

Accuracy is more important than speed on a machine, so take the time to get those curves and shapes smooth and even. As with learning to use a typewriter, your speed will pick up after you learn to use it accurately. If you are not confident using a machine on small or fiddly pieces such as paw pads, then use hand sewing in conjunction with your machine.

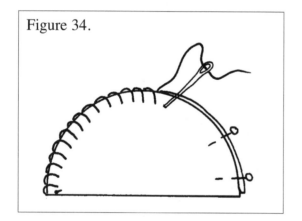

Figure 34.

Hand sewing may be slower but it can often produce a more even curve in a tricky area. It can also be useful to baste your pieces together by hand prior to sewing the seams on a machine. You can do this by using a simple over-and-over stitch called a slipstitch or an overcasting stitch, as in *Fig. 34*. By doing this you have ensured that all the fur is out of the way and not caught in the seam and the pins can be removed before you use the machine. Remember when you baste your pieces together like this not to let your stitches be any deeper than the seam allowance or they will show after the piece is turned through.

If you intend to sew the seam completely by hand after you have overcast your pieces together and removed your pins, you will need to sew in a strong seam of connecting stitches. This can be done using one of several different stitches.

Holbein stitch is simply a reverse running stitch.(*Fig. 35A*) Sewing a running stitch and then turning at the end of the seam and sewing another running stitch back, filling in the gaps left by the first row of stitches, will give you a Holbein stitch. This is a good stitch that produces a strong seam of continuous stitches.

Glover's stitch is really a backstitch. (*Fig. 35B*) This stitch differs slightly from a backstitch in that it is made more like a stab stitch (that is, the needle is taken down and up in separate moves rather than dipped through the fabric) and each stitch connects up with the last. It is this connecting of the stitches that gives you a strong continuous seam. In a normal backstitch the stitches may run parallel to each other but may not interlock with each other, producing a looser seam and one, which can pull apart to show the stitches when the piece is stuffed.

The main thing to remember when hand sewing is to maintain a firm tension so that the stitches will not pull apart after the piece

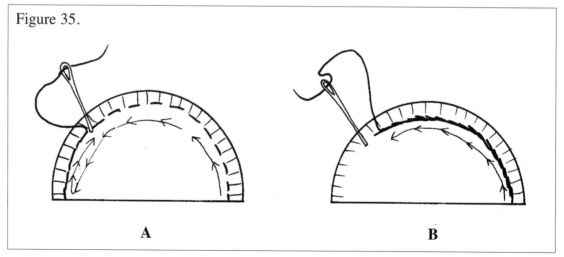

Figure 35.

A

B

is stuffed. If you have a background in embroidery your habit of keeping your stitches looser than is required here may be hard to break! Practice your hand-sewn seams on scraps of fur fabric, turn through and pull apart firmly on the two halves. If you can easily see the stitches try a tighter tension. Pull apart as hard as you can and see if you can rip it. If it does rip it is probably because the seam allowance was not deep enough and the edges of the fabric gave way rather than the stitches. A hand-sewn seam is very strong and rarely comes apart, even under great pressure.

The only other sewing stitch you will need to know is a good closing stitch and that is covered in the Closing and Finishing section.

Sewing the head. As mentioned in the Pinning section above, the head is best started by sewing the chin seam of the two side pieces (see *Fig. 33A*). The head gusset can then be pinned in and sewn. Rather than pinning and sewing one half of the gusset (from the point of the muzzle to the back of the neck) at a time, you may find it better to sew in the U-shape of the muzzle first. Use the reference points you have on your pieces to match it up perfectly. First, find the center of the muzzle end on the head

gusset and pin it into the top of the seam you have just made at the end of the muzzle on the side head pieces. (see *Fig. 36A*). Next, match up the "eye spots" where the muzzle turns into the head. (*Fig. 36B*). Then pin in the "corners" of the muzzle at *Fig. 36C* to ensure that you do not end up sewing a pointed nose. Finally, a pin between points C and B on each side should be enough to hold the muzzle for sewing. By doing this you will make sure that the muzzle is centered correctly and eliminate any possible distortion of the head due to an unevenly sewn-in head gusset.

After the muzzle has been sewn, pin the back end of the head gusset to the bottom edge of the neck on each side (as in *Fig. 37A*) and ease in the pins around the curve of the head. If you find that the gusset is too long, you can trim it down at this stage and make the corresponding change on your pattern.

Once the head is sewn, turn it through and brush it out with your wire brush to remove any fur from the seams. It is a good idea to do this fairly quickly after sewing any body part, as the longer you leave it before brushing the fur out of the seams the more likely it is that the caught fur will be bent and kinked.

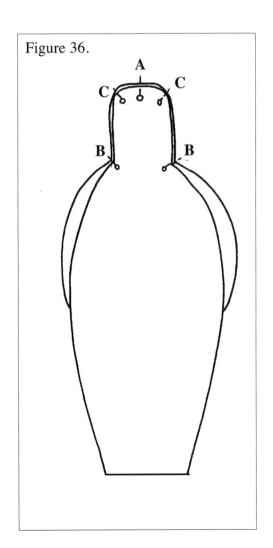

Figure 36.

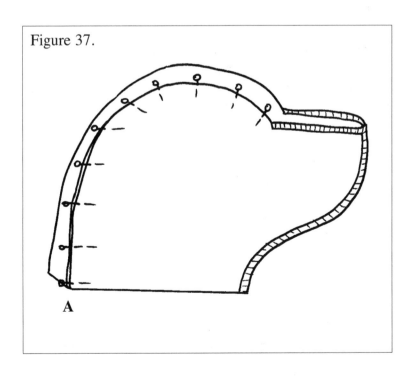

Figure 37.

Sewing the body. If you are working with a two-piece body, the darts will be sewn first, running the seam off into the fabric of the body. (See *Fig. 38A*). The two halves of the body are then pinned and sewn together leaving the back opening. With a four-piece body there are two ways of making it up. You can either sew the front to the back on each side down the side seam (*Fig. 38B*) and then sew down the tummy to the back (leaving the opening as in the back part of *Fig. 38C*), or you can sew the front halves together at the tummy seam and the back halves together (leaving your opening in the middle of the back) before sewing right around the side seam of the body as in *Fig. 38C*.

Make sure that your back opening is large enough for your discs, as well as for anything else you might be putting inside the bear such as a growler or music box. For the neck opening you might choose to sew right over the top of the body and then pierce a hole for the joint, or you may leave a larger hole than you will need (as in *Fig. 38C*) and gather it up before inserting the joint. The advantage of this last method is that it pulls in the top of the body slightly, and may be useful to give a better transition from head to body, particularly if the body is plump.

If the fabric you are working with has a tendency to fray, protect the back opening with either a line of Fray-chek or diluted water-based craft glue along the edges, just in as far as your seam allowance. Once it has dried clear, which only takes five minutes or so, the body can be turned and brushed out. This can be very useful on all openings where joints have to be inserted, but is not essential on ears or heads unless the fabric frays badly.

Sewing the arms. Whether you are using a one-piece arm or a two-piece arm, the paw pad usually gets fitted in and sewn first across the wrist seam. (See *Fig. 39A*). If you are using felt for the paws and you do not want it to stretch or bulge, you can back it first with iron-on interfacing. If you are using excelsior to stuff then this will help prevent the paw pads from looking lumpy. Alternatively, you can use a double layer of felt for the pads.

After sewing in the paw pad the rest of the arm can be sewn, leaving the opening near the joint marker and large enough to take the disc, as in *Fig 39B*. If you have not left a seam allowance for the paw pad you will find that the inner arm is slightly shorter than the outer arm. (Refer back to designing the arm.) Start your pinning from the top of the arm down until you reach the paw pad. Then pin in the center of the tip of the paw pad onto the matching part of the fabric, and ease around the curve on either side. You should be able to fit it in evenly and the end result will be a paw that curves slightly inward.

The sewn arm is then ready for the opening to be edged with your glue solution, let dry and turn.

Sewing the legs. Unlike the arms, with the legs the pad gets put in after the rest of the leg is sewn, as in *Fig. 40*. If you are working with a one-piece leg, then of course the opening will be at the front as the fold is down the back. With a bent leg you might find that the foot is more accessible for stuffing if the opening is on the top of the thigh rather than underneath it.

To facilitate the pinning in of the footpad you could try snipping around the bottom edge of the foot first, not as deep as your seam allowance and about every 1/2in (1cm) or so. Flatten it out and then pin on the footpad. Make sure that the pad is evenly pinned in before sewing. Start with your first pin in the center of the footpad's toe and match it to the center of the toe seam on the leg (See *Fig. 41A*). Then find the center of the heel and pin that into the middle of the heel seam (or the middle of the fold if working with a one-piece leg), as in *Fig. 41B*. Pin in the middle of the

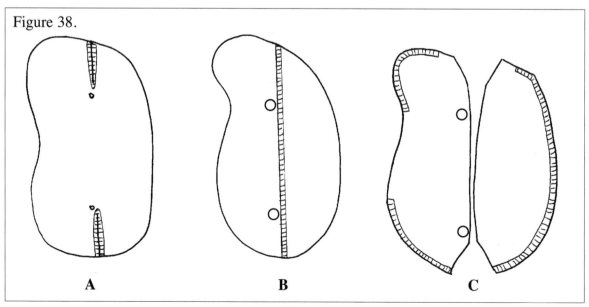

Figure 38.

A   B   C

sides at points C, and if there is a problem with the size of the pad it will show up by this stage.

If it needs to be trimmed down it can either be done to the length or the width, or even both. If it is too small another pad will need to be cut. Whatever changes are made should also be carried out on the pattern so that next time it will be perfect. If the pinning looks good at this stage, finish off with four more pins in between your present ones to hold the pad firmly in place for sewing.

Glue the edges of the leg opening, as with the body and arms, before turning and brushing out.

Sewing the ears. Trimming off the fur in the seam allowance can help make the ears easier to sew with less fur catching in the seam. It can also give a more seamless finish when the ear is turned through. You might also try sewing into the straight edge a little way, as in *Fig. 42A*. This makes the edges easier to sew under once the ear is turned. After turning the ear push the raw edges inside the ear and overcast or ladderstitch it closed, leaving the thread to use for attaching the ear to the head.

Check that both ears have been edged to the same depth, otherwise one ear will be larger than the other. Before sewing them onto the head, try trimming off the fur on the bottom edge and corners, as in *Fig. 42B*. This will make the ear sit more snugly on the head and the flow of the fur will look more natural.

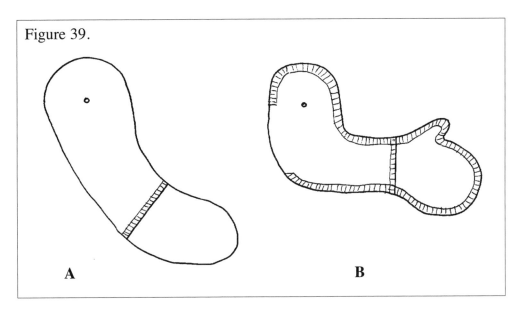

Figure 39.

A   B

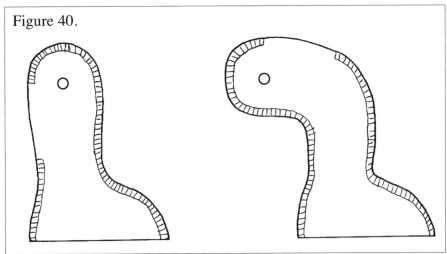

Figure 40.

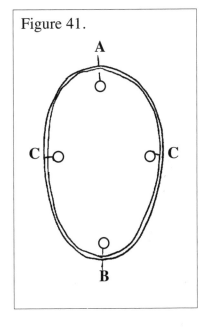

Figure 41.

A

C   C

B

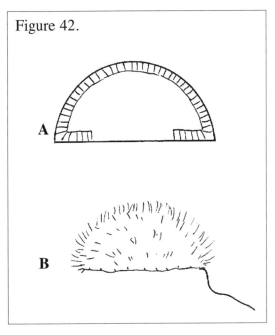

Figure 42.

A

B

55

JOINTING

Once all your pieces are sewn and turned you are ready to joint and stuff. Although the head needs to be stuffed before being jointed and attached to the body, the limbs need to be jointed before stuffing so placing the joints will be discussed before stuffing.

Placing the joints in the limbs. With a brand new pattern you will not be sure if the joint markers you made on the body for the placement of the arms and legs are correct, but this is easy to ascertain once all the sewing is done. The placement of the joints in the limbs should be right, as you calculated the correct size of the disc and the positioning of the joint spot when designing your pattern.

First, place all the joints in the limbs by piercing a hole on the spot marked inside the top of each limb. Make sure that you have a right and a left arm and leg and that you have not marked or sewn together pieces incorrectly. This can happen sometimes with two-piece legs and "teddy baby" style arms as both halves of the limb are similar, and you might have inadvertently sewn two halves with joint marks together leaving one limb with two spots and the other with none!

After you have pierced a suitably large hole with an awl or other sharp, pointed object you can place in the joint. If the hole is a tight fit you may have problems tightening the joint as the fabric can jam in the thread of the bolt or catch in the cotter pin. Make sure that the hole is large enough for the joint shaft to move eas-

ily in and out of it, and push the fabric all the way to the base of the shaft to make sure it is clear. A hole that is not large enough is the cause of most problems in tightening joints, especially when using nuts and bolts.

If you are using cotter pins slide a small washer over one end of the pin and down to the loop before placing another washer over both ends. This first washer will prevent the pin from pulling through the joint as it is tightened. After the second washer place the disc on the pin and push the joint through the hole in the limb from the inside. The shaft of the pin should be the only thing visible from the outside. (See *Fig. 43A*)

For nut and bolt joints also place a washer on the bolt before the disc and then push the joint through the hole. Make sure the fabric is pushed all the way down the shaft and that it is not catching on the thread of the shaft.

Make sure that the disc fits fairly snugly up in the curve of the top of the limb. If there is too much fabric above the disc the stuffed limb will have a bulbous shoulder or hip. If there is not enough fabric the disc will not be able to sit flat and you will have to lower it a little. You should be able to feel an equal amount of fabric all around the top curve of the limb. This will tell you that the joint is placed in centrally and should eliminate potential problems with twisted limbs. All four limbs can have the joints inserted in this way prior to either attaching them to the body or stuffing them.

If you are using Flexlimb, cut the piece slightly shorter than the limb and bend the tip of the wire core into a loop to protect the paw pad. Place the loop over the joint pin or bolt between the washer and the disc, and slide the foam down a little if it gets in the way.

The slit method. This is a way of placing the joints in the limbs after they have been stuffed, and is commonly used on miniature bears. The limbs are sewn completely shut from the outside. A slit is made into the inner half at the top of the limb (where the joint will go) and the limb is turned though the slit. After stuffing, the joint is inserted into the slit and it is then sewn shut, leaving the shaft of the joint sticking out (See *Fig. 43B*). The joint is then attached to the body in the normal way. The advantage of this method is that there is no visible closing seam for the limbs, and this can be helpful when using the upholstery velvets for miniature bears, as the short pile tends to show up any external stitches.

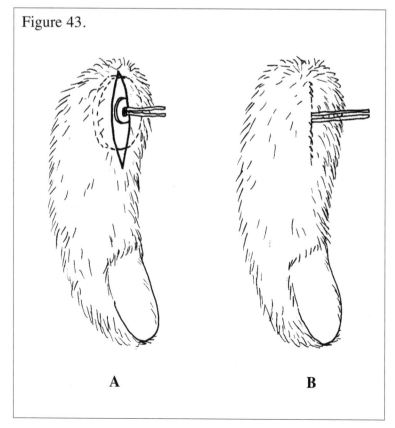

Figure 43.

A   B

56

Jointing the limbs to the body. Now that all the limbs have their joints inside them they can be attached to the body. If you are working with a new design then you may be unsure where they will be positioned. As long as you have some arm and leg spots marked inside the body as reference points it is quite easy to determine their exact location.

Start with the legs as they are easier. Find the leg spot you marked inside the body and push a pin through the spot to the outside of the body. Hold up the appropriate leg with the shaft of the joint against the pin. (Alternatively you can hold the tip of your finger against the spot on the inside of the body and put the end of the joint shaft against it from the outside). Have a look at the leg and how it relates to the body from the side, the front and in a sitting position.

If there is too large a distance between the inside edge of the leg and the center seam at the base of the body (see *Fig. 44A*) the leg will be too high and the bear will end up with very wide hips. When seen in a sitting position this type of bear will be seen to be sitting on the base of its body rather than the back of its thighs.

If there is too little space between the inside edge of the leg and the center seam under the body the legs will be too close together and may even cross over each other rather than stand properly. If you try to sit such a bear you will find that the legs also open out very wide and the bear tends to fall over as it has no base to sit on.

Ideally there should be enough room between the legs so that they hang straight and do not cross, although they may touch at the ankle. When the bear is seated and viewed from the side or back he should be seen to be resting on both the base of the body and the back of the legs.

When you are happy with the position of the leg, poke a hole through the body at that spot for the joint shaft. If you find that your reference spot was not quite where it should have been, your hole may be slightly higher or lower than it. Using the distance from the reference spot to your new hole, match up the other leg. (This is where having those reference spots is so handy, as now both legs will be even with no guesswork involved.) Go back to your pattern and correct the position on the body piece so that in future the leg spots will be in the right position.

Push the shaft of the joint all the way in, making sure that the hole is large enough, and inside the body place another disc on the shaft followed by another washer. If you are using cotter pins roll down the two ends inside the body (with either a cotter pin

key or a pair of needle-nosed pliers) away from each other until they are snugly against the washer. (See *Fig. 30B*).

If you are using bolts, place your locknut on the shaft and finger-tighten until it stops turning, which means that the nylon insert has reached the thread. Pinch the discs together to check that no fabric is jamming between them and push them against the head of the bolt in the leg. Placing a nut driver over the head of the bolt inside the leg, hold it still and tighten down the nut inside the body with either another nut driver or a ratchet spanner/wrench. (See *Fig. 30C*) Tighten it down as hard as you can and then loosen it off half a turn.

Check the movement of the joint. It should be firm enough so that the empty leg does not swing, and in fact should be able to be moved only by holding the edges of the two discs and turning them against each other. If the limb moves too easily when it is empty, by the time it is stuffed it will be too loose as the limb will act as a lever. If you intend to stuff firmly then the limbs should be firmer than for a very softly stuffed bear. Practice will give you the feel of the right tightness for the joints, and using locknuts gives you the opportunity to play around with adjusting them. Be careful with overworking cotter pins as they can get metal fatigue and break off.

Once you are happy with the tension of your first joint then keep referring back to that one as you tighten the other joints, so that all limbs have the same ease of movement.

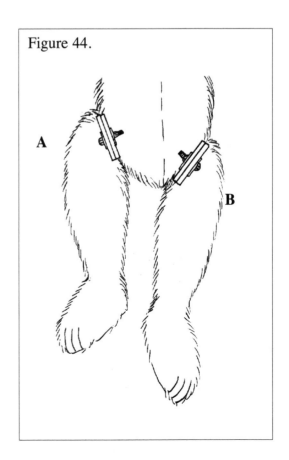

Figure 44.

Jointing the arms to the body can also be done at this stage, but it important to remember that if you have gathered the fabric around the neck for the head joint then you will be affecting the positioning of the arms, perhaps to an unknown degree if this is a new design. Even if you are just poking a hole for the head joint into the sewn seams at the top of the body the disc will take up a fair bit of that space.

You can calculate how much by placing a disc over where the head joint will go and seeing how much space you have between the edge of the disc and the arm hole (stick a pin through the hole from the inside). Alternatively you could joint the stuffed head on to the body before jointing on the arms. Place the arm with its joint shaft against the pin and see how much room there will be between the top of the shoulder and the edge of the neck (disc). There should be at least a finger's width between the two (on a 10in [25cm] bear) or the bear will look as though he has no neck or is shrugging his shoulders. As with the legs, once you have determined the correct position of the arm spot, use the original reference spot to guide you for the other arm and make any necessary alterations to the original pattern.

Jointing the head. The head will need to be stuffed before placing in the neck joint, unless you are using a pattern which leaves a hole in the head to stuff through and joints it to the body before stuffing, but this is an unusual procedure. See the following section on stuffing for the head.

When the head is ready to be jointed the stuffing will firmly and evenly fill the muzzle, head and neck but will not protrude from the neck opening. If the neck is very short and gathering the neck fabric in around the joint will result in no neck at all, make a reminder for yourself on the pattern for next time, then cut a circle of matching fur fabric slightly smaller than the disc. Prepare a joint with a cotter pin or bolt then a washer and a disc. Poke a hole in the center and push in down the shaft of the joint until the fabric is against the underside of the disc. Hold the head upside down and place the circle on it with the shaft of the disc standing straight up (see *Fig. 45A*) and lace the edges of the neck together with a strong thread using a ladder stitch. Because the circle is slightly smaller than the disc the seam should pull in underneath the neck and will not be visible once the head is on the body.

Another way of covering the base of the neck is to leave the head gusset extra long and with a semicircular end. It is then folded under the neck (poking the joint shaft through the middle of it first) and sewn around the edges to close the neck with the joint in place.

If the neck looks a suitable length, with a strong thread gather around the edge, place in the joint as in *Fig. 45B* and pull it tight. If you cannot completely cover the disc by this method alone, then continue with your thread and stitch across the neck in a star-shaped pattern pulling each stitch tight until the edges are drawn in around the shaft of the joint. Knot off several times to anchor it securely.

The head is now ready to be jointed to the body. If you are using nuts and bolts for jointing there are a number of ways to joint the head. This is not as simple as jointing the arms and legs, because the head of the bolt needs to be held still while the nut is tightened and this cannot be done on the stuffed head, where the head of the bolt is inside the head cavity.

You could solve this dilemma by using a cotter pin joint for the neck and locknuts and bolts for the limbs. Alternatively, you could try using superglue to attach the bolt head to the washer and disc before putting it in the head. This can prevent shifting and enable a locknut to be used in the neck joint. Or you could try using two nuts on the neck joint, an ordinary hexagonal nut and a locknut. After tightening down the ordinary nut it is held still with a spanner or wrench while the locknut is tightened on top of it. Yet another solution is to use one ordinary nut, tighten it down until you are satisfied with the movement of the head, and then dribble a drop of superglue down into the thread of the nut. Hold the bear upside down for several minutes while the superglue dries and you have created your own locknut on the neck. (There are several products available from hardware shops, such as Loctite, which do the same thing.)

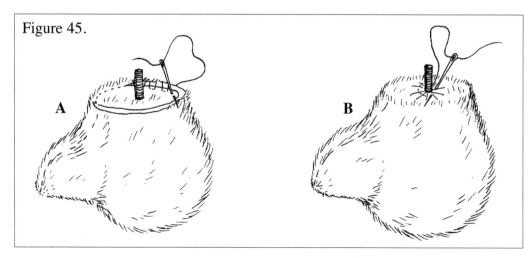

Figure 45.

A

B

STUFFING

Excelsior or wood wool was the earliest type of teddy bear stuffing and was packed in firmly to produce a hard, not very cuddly bear. Over time the wood wool tended to break down into sawdust giving the old bears saggy tummies and nodding heads. Excelsior is still used by Steiff for their collectors' range of white tag limited edition bears and also by some bear artists. It can be used alone or in conjunction with another type of stuffing. Some bear makers use excelsior in the muzzle as they find it easier to sew the nose and mouth. Others use it in the wrists and ankles to strengthen them.

Excelsior can be found in several grades, from the cheap packing wood wool to the type made expressly for bear stuffing. The quality excelsior is more readily obtainable in Europe than elsewhere. It is finely stranded and comes in sealed boxes so that it retains its natural oils and suppleness. It should be used as soon as possible after opening, or the oils dry out and it becomes stiff to work with.

If you can only find a poorer quality wood wool try dampening it first with a water spray pump before use. Keep it in a sealed plastic bag to prevent it from drying out but take care that it does not rot.

Stuffing with excelsior can be hard on the hands. It is used by either rolling it into a ball or pulling it into strands and folding it in with a large forked stuffing tool. A wooden spoon handle with a notch cut in it can work well.

Kapok is from the seed pods of a large tropical tree and was the second type of stuffing used in bears. Steiff experimented with it early on in the development of bears as it was lighter and softer than excelsior. Its dustiness and allergenic properties make it an unpopular choice for bear makers these days. It also tends to "wad" or pack down into lumps and can be difficult to use because of this.

Cotton is another natural fiber and clean ginned cotton has similar qualities to kapok, but without the dust. It can be useful for stuffing small or miniature bears if you want a firmly packed bear.

Flax and **copra** are some other natural plant fibers that can be used in stuffing. Flax is like a very fine excelsior and can work well in tiny bears where an excelsior look and feel is wanted. Copra is also fibrous but heavier in texture and not as malleable for stuffing.

Wool can be a great stuffing material and cleaned raw fleece can be a cheap resource if you are in a rural area with sheep. Due to its resilience, wool makes for a springy stuffing and is good for a softly stuffed bear.

Pellets are small plastic beads originally used by the doll makers to weight doll bodies. They can also be effectively used in stuffing bears when used in conjunction with another filler, such as polyfill. Pellets come in different sizes and qualities, so make sure they are the type that slides and not the sticky ones. Some types also smell quite strongly and should be avoided. Tiny pellets are also now available for small bears, and also come in glass as well as plastic.

As the pellets are heavy they add a nice weight to a bear, but they should be used in moderation. If the body and limbs and completely stuffed with pellets they will not hold their shape, particularly in the upper portions like the shoulders and hips. Also when pellets are used in the paw area the pads have a dimpled look and crunchy feel. If too many pellets are used the bear feels hard and crunchy, rather like a full sack of rice.

It is necessary to stuff the limbs and body first with polyfill, as in *Fig. 46*, leaving a cavity in the middle of each section. Sew the

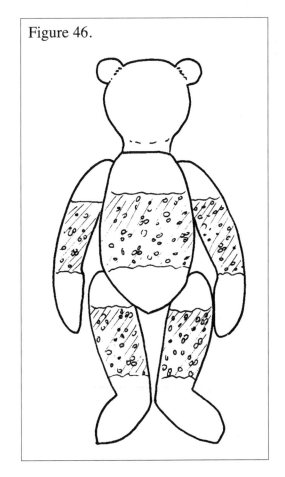

Figure 46.

closing seam about three-quarters closed, leaving a hole just big enough to take a funnel. This will prevent the pellets from spilling out as you use them. A metal funnel tends to let the pellets slide in better than a plastic one (make sure that the funnel hole is big enough for the pellets), or try a large nozzle piping syringe without the plunger. It can also be a good idea to place the bear in a baking tray or new kitty litter tray to catch any escaping pellets.

Use less pellets than you think you will need and blend them in with small loose balls of polyfill to achieve a soft, huggable filling without feeling the pellets. Pellets should not be used in the head and growlers should not be used in the bodies of pellet-filled bears as the growler will shift and be felt through the fabric. If you want to use a growler in a pellet-filled bear, try putting it in the head!

Polyfill is the most commonly used filling for all modern toys, as well as for cushions, pillows, and upholstered furniture. It is a man-made fiber and comes in many different grades which are useful for different types of stuffing. A coarser, cheaper quality polyfill will have a slightly harsh feel to it and will pack down well to give a good firm stuffing. At the other end of the polyfill range is a type of superfluff that is light and silky, its bounciness makes it great for a softly filled bear but it is hard to pack down firmly. Often different types of polyfill are used in the one bear to achieve different effects.

STUFFING TIPS

- Make sure that you have left your openings to be accessible for stuffing to the farthest and most difficult to reach places, and make sure that you stuff these places first.
- Always keep feeling for lumps and dips with your hands as you stuff, and "sculpt" the piece as you go, pushing and rolling it to get the shape you want.
- Try to layer your stuffing to avoid lumps, and don't be too fussy about placing each piece of stuffing or it will take forever. Keep packing it in and move it around with your stuffing tool once it starts to take shape.
- Place a large loose ball of stuffing in the center cavity of the head while you concentrate on stuffing the nose. This will help prevent the nose stuffing from popping back into the head.

- Even if you want a softly stuffed bear, make sure that the head is firmly stuffed and that there is adequate stuffing over the joints, both inside the body and inside the limbs.
- Soft-stuff the eye sockets when stuffing the head to enable the eyes to be pulled in further, giving better character.
- Try excelsior in the muzzle to make it easier to sew the nose.
- If you are using an armature (LocLine, Flexlimb or even pipe cleaners) remember to stuff loosely to allow movement. The same is also true when stuffing bent limbs in order to make them more poseable.
- Stitch through the hump to keep the stuffing in place in a softly stuffed bear, or in a pellet-filled bear.
- Try combinations of stuffings for different effects.

NEEDLE-SCULPTING

This is a fairly new innovation and one that can be used to give the bear's character a whole new dimension. Basically it involves stitching through the head in a variety of ways, before the eyes are put in or the nose is embroidered. Using a long needle and a strong thread (a thin strand of the artificial sinew works well), small stitches are taken in the area of the face that you want to manipulate, pulled in and secured. It is like plastic surgery for teddy bears!

Look at your blank, stuffed head (with the joint inserted) and decide if anything needs improving. Perhaps the bridge of the nose is too wide, or the eye sockets not defined enough, maybe his cheeks need a little more plumpness or he could do with worried eyebrows. There are a lot of ways of increasing facial expression with just a few stitches in the right places. Ears can also be changed in various ways with needle sculpture.

The head has to be a blank canvas otherwise an embroidered nose would buckle and eyes would loosen if needle sculpting was performed afterwards. The head also has to have some resilience in the fabric and stuffing which means that it cannot be rock hard. If it is too hard there is a chance that the seams of the head might split, so if you plan to needle sculpt a head stuff it bearing this in mind (excuse the pun.)

If you find it hard to visualize where the nose and eyes will be, use pins or tacked threads to assist you. To start your needle sculpting, bring your thread up from the edge of the neck disc leaving your knot where it will be covered when the head is attached to the body. (Also finish in the same way.) Bring the needle out to where you want to start.

To define and deepen the eye sockets bring your needle out near where you will be placing the eye. Take a small stitch through to

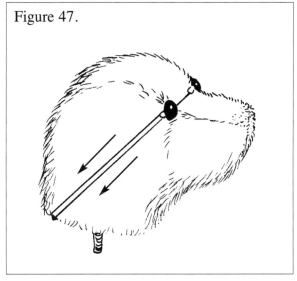

Figure 47.

Figure 48.

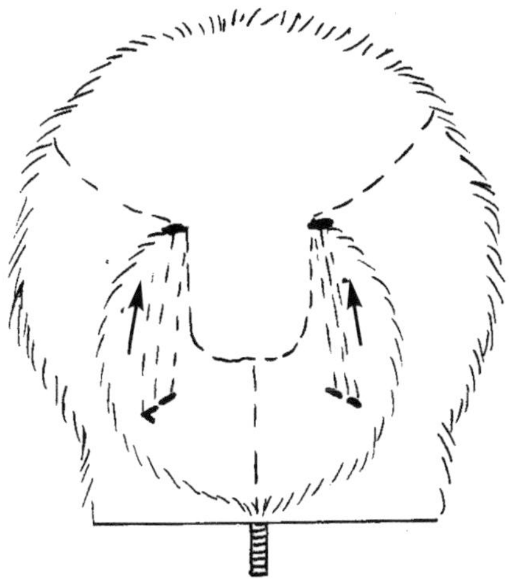

the back of the base of the neck and another back up to near your first stitch. Continue in this way, pulling tightly with each stitch, until you make a small circle of stitches around the point where you intend to sink the eye. (See *Fig. 47*) Keep the circle small enough so that the eye will cover it. Finish off by knotting at the base of the neck.

To enhance the smile bring your needle out where you will be placing the eye, take a small stitch and take the needle out to where the end of the mouth line will be on the same side of the face (use pins to calculate this if necessary.) Take a small stitch and go back up to the same eye and pull tight, as in *Fig 48*. A dimple should appear and the end of the mouth will lift. Repeat on the other side, then knot off at the base of the neck.

To bring the eyes closer together bring your needle out near where the eye will go and take a small stitch, bringing your needle out at the other eye socket. Repeat and go back to the first side, pulling tight on each stitch, as in *Fig. 49*. Do not go into the same spot twice or you may rip the fabric and try not to catch up your threads inside the head. The best way to avoid this is to make your stitches in a short row on either side of the nose. Once the nose has pulled in to the right extent finish off in the usual way.

To lift the bridge of the nose continue the steps above but take your row of stitches further down the sides of the nose near the seam edges. This will have the effect of narrowing the top of the head gusset on the muzzle by pinching it up. The stitches can be used down part or all of the nose, depending on the look you want to achieve.

To form eyebrow ridges bring your needle out above the eye

socket and make two small rows of stitches much like ladder stitch, as in *Fig. 50*. Pull them together as you go and the fabric will rise between the rows to form a brow. Repeat on the other side and finish off as usual.

Ear sculpting is done after the ears are sewn in position and is usually performed as a treatment for imperfect ears. If the ear needs to be cupped more, take a little stitch at the top and the bottom of the ear and pull them together. A stitch or two at the top of the ear can be used to lift an ear slightly, and a few tiny stitches at the bottom edge can be used to pull down the ear. In this way you can often even out slightly mismatched ears without having to remove them.

Toe sculpting is fun on contemporary looking bears and is done after the leg is stuffed. The paws need to be large and not too tightly stuffed. Using your long needle and a strong thread

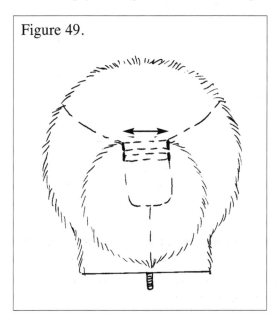

Figure 49.

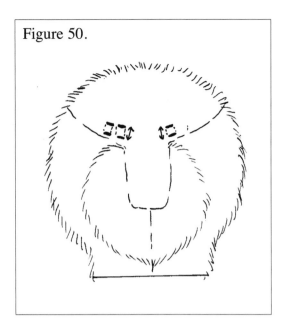

Figure 50.

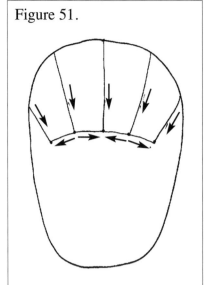

Figure 51.

(nylon line or a close color match to the paw pad material is a good idea) take long stitches down into the paw pad, as in *Fig. 51* and pull up tightly. Make the number of pads you want then secure a tight knot. If you wish you can also edge the bottom of the pads by putting in stitches which pull away from each other, as illustrated.

EYES

Boot buttons were used on the first teddy bears and antique boot buttons or shoe buttons are now still available in limited quantities and sizes. They were made of compressed and molded wood pulp in a hemispherical shape with metal loops or shanks set into the flat backs. Sometimes they are also found in a flatter form. Although they were made in black, brown, gray, and even white, it is the black ones that are commonly found in bears. They are very strong and it is rare to find them broken even in old teddy bears. The soft sheen of the curved surface is very attractive and imparts a special look to a bear. They are available from some bear makers' suppliers, usually in the 8, 9 and 10mm sizes, although originally they were made from 5mm (for dolls' shoes) up to 14mm or so. The large sizes are now available again as reproduction boot buttons in the USA.

Glass eyes with pupils were introduced to the teddy bear industry around 1908 and the first type tended to be of clear glass with painted enamel backs on wire stalks. Shortly afterwards the popular amber glass eyes with pupils appeared. Both types of glass eyes in many sizes and colors are readily available to the teddy bear maker today, with either wire stalks or wire loop backs. As these eyes are hand blown they tend to vary in size and shape. Not only does the iris of the eye vary but the pupil may also vary so it is necessary to match them carefully before use. Take care that the pupil is not offset or the bear may end up looking cross-eyed or wall-eyed! You can match up eyes by pushing them into Styrofoam, Plasticine or card.

If you cannot find a color that matches your bear, try painting your own custom eyes. Buy the clear glass ones with pupils and use small pots of model enamel paints on the backs of the eyes. Try a combination of colors, or layer them for greater depth.

Black glass eyes are possibly more commonly used than colored ones by bear makers these days because the black eye is easier to match without that pupil and the eye looks more like the old boot buttons. They come in a huge range of sizes and you can even try antiquing them to look more like boot buttons.

Antiqued glass eyes are simply made by lightly brushing the surface of the glass eye with very fine sandpaper. This dulls the sheen and gives the softer look of the old boot button. It is great when you are working with a sized eye that is not available as a boot button but you want the antique look.

Safety eyes are used in most countries in children's' toys as they meet the safety standard requirements, while the glass sewn-in eyes do not. They are made of plastic or perspex and look like a mushroom. A metal-toothed ring fits onto the shaft of the mushroom and locks it in place. Rather than being pulled into the head after it is stuffed, as the glass eyes are, the safety eye is fitted in the empty head. The main disadvantage to this is that the eye tends to sit on the surface rather than in an eye socket so the head may lack definition and the bear may lack character.

The safety eye is by no means completely safe either, and the metal-toothed ring has been known to saw through the shaft of the eye, which then falls out. Safety eyes are not commonly used by individual bear makers who are creating bears for the adult collector rather than for children but it is important to let the public know if that is the case. (See Business section.)

Putting in sewn-in eyes is very simple, but first you have to decide whether your bear is young or old, and whether it is male or female. Amazing but true, the size of the eyes and their positioning can determine sex and age. Young bears and female bears tend to have larger eyes than older bears, and male bears tend to have eyes that are closer together than female bears. Baby bears will also tend to have their eyes quite low in their heads which accentuates their larger, rounder heads.

Putting in the eyes can be done when the head is stuffed and has the neck joint in place, but before it is attached to the body and even before it has a nose. Alternatively, it can be the last thing you do to finish off your bear. Your sequence of events in making a bear will be determined by what works for you and can be a very personal thing. Some people feel that the bear "comes alive" once it has its eyes so they should be done last. Others feel that you get a better finish by being able to hide the knots under the neck if you put the eyes in before the head is on the body. Some people put the eyes in before the nose, others cannot visualize what sized eyes should be used unless they sew in the nose first.

Whatever your sequence of events is, when you are ready to put in the eyes their positioning can be worked out using drawing pins or pins with a circle of black felt in the appropriate size. When you are happy with the position (which is usually at the base of the muzzle - the "eye spot" - and close to the seam but either inside or outside it. Never put the eyes right into the seams as they could split) carefully match up a pair of eyes of the right size. There are many different ways of putting in eyes but this is possibly the simplest, where the eye threads are taken through to the back of the base of the neck and knotted together. It is also possible to sew in the eyes on one thread or to cross the threads in order to pull the eyes closer together as you tighten up before knotting.

Using a long doll needle (long enough to go diagonally through the head) and a long length of strong thread or artificial sinew, place one eye on a thread and put both ends in through the eye of the needle so that the eye is hanging on a loop. If you want to you can knot the eye in place on its threads. Check that the wire loop at the back of the eye is standing up straight and has not been bent as this can affect how the eye sits in the head. It is a good idea to pinch shut the wire loop with a pair of pliers as this will reduce the size of the hole you have to make in order to sink the eye. You will find that this is not possible if you are using old boot buttons as the metal shank loops are too heavy to pinch closed; instead you will just have to make a larger hole.

With an awl or other sharp, pointed implement poke a hole in where your pins were marking the eye positions. Take your needle in through the hole and out at the back of the base of the neck, as low as possible. Some people put eye threads through to where the ears will be, knot them off there and then cover the knot by sewing on the ears. If the head is not very hard or if you want to pull the eyes

in very firmly, this way of placing in the eyes can lead to distortion of the head at the knots.

Talcum powder on the long needle can help it slip through the head more easily. It is likely that you will feel the needle slide off the edge of the disc. Pull on the threads and make sure that the eye is in. Remove your needle and let the threads hang. Rethread your needle with the other eye and prepare it as before. Place in the other eye and bring out about 1/4in (.31cm) away from the first threads. (If you come out of the same hole as the first threads and knot them together the knot will sink deep inside the head with the pressure from the eyes and the eyes may loosen.) Check that each eye is in and use your needle to pull out any fur that has been caught behind the eyes.

Try using a leather finger stall or wearing an old leather glove when pulling in and knotting eyes to protect against cut fingers. Make a half knot of the two sets of threads with each other as in *Fig. 52.* Going over more than once can help stop it slipping as you tighten in the eyes, particularly if you are not using artificial sinew. If you are using the sinew you will find that its stickiness will help hold your half knot at this stage.

Now for the isometric workout — pull as hard as you can on the eyes to sink them in nicely. It can even help to have someone pushing on the eyes from the other side of the head and that can often take the strain off the eyes making them less likely to break. If they do break, and the glass eyes do sometimes come off their wires, especially if they are small or the wire does not have much depth in the glass they will probably do so now and not normally once the eyes have been in place for a while. The boot buttons very rarely break.

When you are happy that the eyes are even (look down from the top of the head as well as from the front) and in far enough, finish off your knot tightly and knot over it again to be sure that it is secure. Thread up all your threads on the doll needle (you should be able to do it in one go) and sink the knot by taking the needle down right next to the knot and bringing it out somewhere else at the base of the neck. Give it a tug and the knot should sink down out of sight. The threads can then be cut off close to the fabric. All external knots should be sunk and hidden in this way.

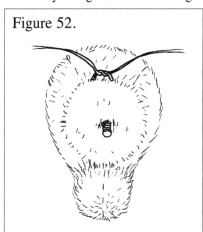

Figure 52.

NOSES

Preparation. Before deciding what type of nose you want to make for your bear you need to determine the right position for it, and this may not be as obvious as you think. What will the angle of the head be once the head is on the body? Do you want his muzzle to appear longer or shorter, should it be tipped up or drooping down? How long should the septum stitch be connecting the nose to the mouth? How much depth of muzzle do you have when looking at the head from the side?

Muzzle depth is the first thing you will need to check, as in *Fig. 53*. Illustration A shows a bear with a deep muzzle, B has an average muzzle and C has a shallow muzzle. Each of these bears will look its best with the nose positioned in a different way.

When you look at a bear face to face you want to see his face; his eyes looking at you, his nose twitching in your direction and the expression in his mouth. If the muzzle is shallow and the nose is below the tip (and the horizontal seam at the end of the muzzle) as in *Fig. 56B*, the mouth may end up underneath the jaw and not be visible from the front at all. To counteract a mouse-like muzzle, the nose might be better situated above the horizontal end seam and have a short septum line connecting it to the mouth, as in *Fig. 56A*. This would make the mouth visible from the front and make the best use of a shallow muzzle.

If the bear has a very deep muzzle, however, you really cannot place the nose in the same way as you would for the bear with a shallow muzzle. If you do, and have the nose above the horizon-tal end seam, as in *Fig. 54A*, you will end up with a bear with a very heavy jaw. One way of avoiding this is to make the septum stitch longer to take up most of the muzzle depth; the other is to drop the positioning of the nose below the horizontal seam, as in *Fig. 54B*.

If your bear has a nicely balanced muzzle depth then you have more options to play with when deciding on where to position the nose, but it often looks best when evenly placed halfway over the horizontal seam, as in *Fig. 55A*. This spot will be able to give more curve to the nose shape as well by using the angle of the muzzle's tip.

In general the width of the nose will be decided by the width of the nose section on the head gusset. The embroidered nose will tend to look best if it takes up most or all of that gusset width, as in *Fig. 55B*. If it is too narrow it can look a little mean and ratty, if it is too wide it will extend past the edges of the gusset and drop down the sides of the nose which may not give the desired look.

Once you have decided on the placement of the nose it is necessary to clear away the fur from the area by trimming it right down to the fabric base. This is not the final trimming for the muzzle and if you have not yet decided how you are going to trim the face it is important not to take off too much, only enough for the nose to be stitched. If you know that the muzzle will be almost entirely shaved anyway, take off more than the nose area

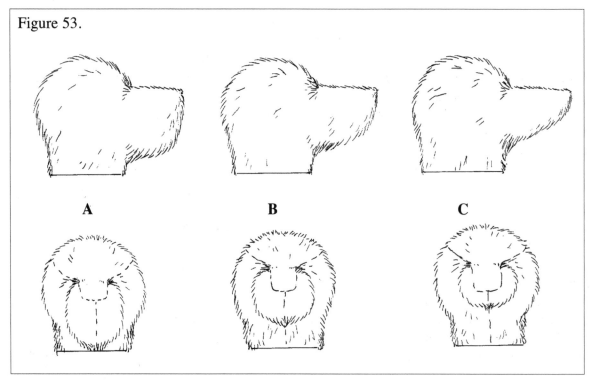

Figure 53.

A   B   C

to make the nose easier and clearer to sew. By clearing away the fur on the nose area you will be making it easier to stitch the nose and also prevent any fur from poking through the stitches.

Shapes. There are as many different nose shapes as you can think of and they can be made in a variety of ways other than stitching. Historically the first Steiff bears' noses were not stitched but were made of gutta percha, a type of black sealing wax. Although they were shiny and realistically shaped with nostrils, they tended to shatter and were quickly replaced with more durable stitched noses.

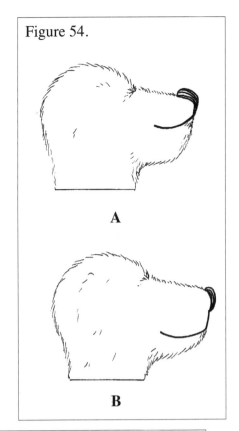

Figure 54.

Steiff then adopted two styles of embroidered noses, which they still use today, making horizontally stitched noses for their smaller bears and vertically stitched noses for the larger bears. The larger bears in the early years also had a felt template under the stitching.

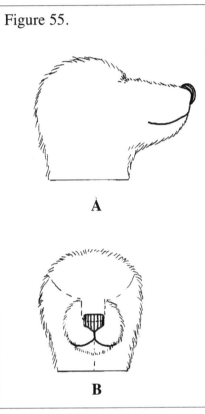

Figure 55.

Many soft toy manufacturers developed particular stitching styles for their bear' noses and even though they often employed a vertically stitched nose the small differences between them can be used to help identify old bears today. Steiff's vertical nose looks like *Fig. 57A*, while Bing's had a stitch lining the lower edge of the nose, as in *Fig. 57B*. The Hermann company adopted a long stitch extending below the outer edges of the nose, as in *Fig. 57C*, while the English company Farnell used a long stitch extending above the outer edges of the nose as in *Fig. 57D*. Many modern bear artists have also developed their own signature style of bear nose, which may be embroidered, modeled or even carved from a variety of substances. *Fig. 58* shows a variety of different stitched noses that are popular, but why not make up your own?

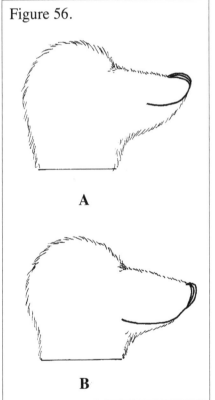

Figure 56.

Outlines can often be helpful in working out the size and positioning of the nose. This can be done using **pins** (*Fig. 59A*), **stitches** (*Fig. 59B*), drawing lines with a permanent or fade-out marker, or a glued on **template** (*Fig. 59C*). A template can be made from scraps of felt or leather and cut into the shape you want for the nose and then glued into place with a tacky contact cement. You might find that a firmer leather template will work better than a thinner felt which may roll or buckle as you stitch. You can even try padding the template by stuffing underneath it. A padded leather or suede nose may be what you want to use and

Figure 57.

Figure 58.

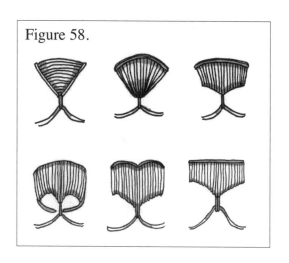

details such as sculpted nostrils can add a nice touch. Fray-chek on the muzzle can stiffen it prior to stitching and may make it easier to work with. Once you are happy with your outline you are ready to stitch your nose.

The main things to remember when stitching a nose are to maintain a strong, even tension on the stitches and to keep the stitches as close together as possible. If you are using a double strand of thread then you can prevent them from twisting by taking your needle between the threads as you make each stitch.

If the muzzle is not firmly and evenly stuffed you may find that the stitches can distort the nose, so ensure that your stuffing is perfect before you start. If you are concerned that the stitching may shift the stuffing in the muzzle, then leave the neck open until after the nose is stitched. You then have the option of adding more stuffing or re-positioning any stuffing that may have shifted during stitching, before putting the neck joint in and closing off the neck opening.

Figure 59.

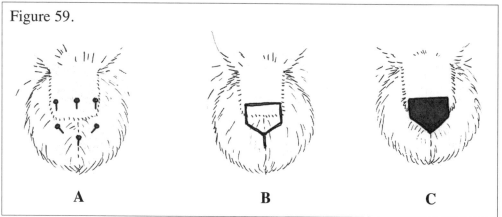

A   **B**   **C**

Horizontal. A horizontally stitched nose is probably the easiest type of nose to work with and has several advantages. It does not need an outline as the seams on the gusset provide the outline. (See *Fig. 60A*) It can be edged smoothly with one stitch running under the septum stitch, as in *Fig. 60B*, and the mouth can also be formed with one stitch running under the septum as in *Fig. 60C*.

Figure 60.

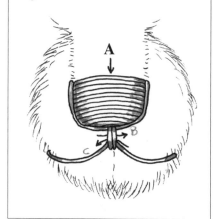

Vertical. A vertically stitched nose often incorporates the septum stitch into the central stitches of the nose, as in *Fig. 61*. In this case the mouth stitch cannot be looped behind the septum, as it can in the horizontally stitched nose. This is because if the septum stitch forms part of the nose it will be pulled down by the mouth stitch and may ruin the smooth surface of the stitched nose. The mouth will be made in two stitches, using as a center the spot below the septum (which should also be lined up with the seam that runs under the chin).

Figure 61.

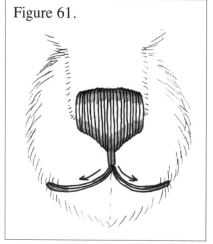

The stitches for the nose can be made coming down from the top of the nose or coming up from the bottom of the nose, whichever you find more comfortable. The nose can also be edged with a

66

long satin stitch along the top and underneath if you are unhappy with the regularity of your stitches. This is a good way of giving a neat finish and hiding any small imperfections.

The stitches can either be worked out from the center septum line one at a time on either side, or one side can be finished and then the other. You may find that doing one stitch a side at a time can build up the stitches at the back of the nose and make it hard to get the needle through, in which case stitching half a nose at a time (as in *Fig. 62*) may work better for you.

Templates. If you are using a template underneath your stitching, you will need to make sure that the stitches not only maintain the tension but actually increase in tension as you approach the outer edge of the template (see *Fig. 62*). This will help to pull the edges of the template down to the level of the fabric and by the time your stitches reach the edge there will not be a ledge to "drop off". (This ledge can also be removed to some extent by paring down the edges before gluing the template in position.)

It is important also to ensure that your stitches stay clear of the template, and do not come up underneath its top or bottom edge. If this does happen you will find that the template is actually lifted off the nose or rolled under itself and the shape of the nose will be deformed. It is a good practice to keep your line of stitches slightly above and below the edges of the template, as in the dotted line of *Fig. 63*.

Molded leather. A leather nose can be either stitched or glued in place. It can be made up of several layers of leather or suede and stuffed or molded into shape. Some very lifelike noses can be achieved in this way.

Waxed noses. Waxing has become popular recently for stitched noses, as it produces a good luster and can give a very smooth surface to the nose. It is simply done by melting a small quantity of beeswax in a double boiler on the stove or in a microwave (it can be slow to melt) and quickly applying it to the nose before it hardens with an old paintbrush or with a cotton bud (Q-tip) or sponge-tip makeup applicator. The wax is then buffed with either an old toothbrush or, for a smoother finish, with a piece of paper. Excess wax can be melted and even evaporated by applying heat again. (Try using a hairdryer!)

It can be a good idea to isolate the nose prior to waxing by surrounding it with strips of transparent sticky tape in order to prevent wax from clogging the fur around the nose.

Other finishes such as resin or varnish are sometimes used to produce an extra shine to an embroidered nose and can be used in layers to build up the polish of the nose.

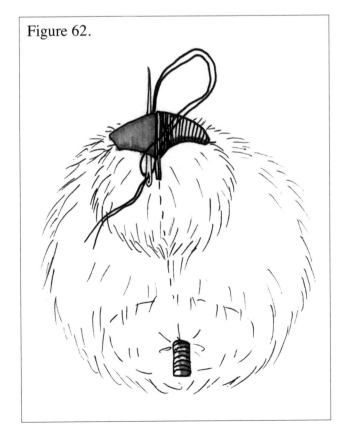

Figure 62.

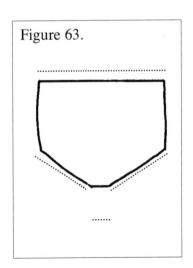

Figure 63.

CLOSING AND FINISHING

Start your closing seam with a strong knotted thread, brought up inside and slightly above the top edge of the opening. It is a good idea to overlap the last few stitches of the seam at both ends of the opening to ensure that there are no gaps in your closing seam. Use the same seam allowance as the rest of your sewing and make sure that the edges are fray-checked or stiffened with the craft glue solution if the fabric looks like fraying.

About halfway down the seam check that no more stuffing is needed in the piece you are working on. To knot off at the end of the seam, pick up a thread from an "old" stitch inside the seam and make your knot over that. Take your needle down inside the seam and bring it out elsewhere, giving it a tug to sink the knot inside the seam.

It can be a good idea to start your closing from the top of each piece and work down in the same direction as the fur. This makes it easier to tuck in the edges of the fabric as well as to see where you are placing your stitches.

French Lacing Stitch used to be the most common way of closing seams on bears after stuffing them. Basically a herringbone shape, the stitches are made in a zigzag pattern, as in *Fig. 64A*. It is easy to do but the stitches remain visible in the seam. The early bears often had this method of closing and the final body seam was usually on the tummy.

Ladder Stitch is a better way to close seams as it produces an invisible seam by pulling the stitches down into the seam itself. It is made by stitching across the opening and then taking a small stitch down the same side before going across and repeating it on the other side (see *Fig. 64B*). It is important to keep the stitches

parallel, otherwise the edges of the fabric can pucker, and if the stitches cross each other it will not work effectively.

Pull the stitches in after every two or three "rungs of the ladder" are made across the opening, by making sure that the edges are tucked under, pinching them together and pulling the thread. If you make too many stitches before pulling the seam closed there is a chance that you may strain and snap the thread.

Ladder stitch is a very useful stitch and can be used to great effect in repairing old bears or doing any work where it is necessary to work from the outside. Some miniature bears are sewn entirely from the right side using ladder stitch.

Trimming on the head can really bring out the character of the bear as well as sculpting its features. Trimming can be done with many different tools, including lint shavers, electric clippers, shavers and scissors. The tools you use will depend on the effect you want. Shavers and electric clippers can be fast and useful if you want to trim a larger area, or right back to the fabric backing. Scissors will be slower but can give you a better-graduated cut and more subtle variation in fur length. Always use small scissors with fine, sharp points as large scissors will not give you the maneuverability you will need for delicate work.

To avoid any visible cut marks in the fur, always cut with the grain of the fur, that is, always keep the tips of the scissors in the same direction as the tips of the fur. (The scissors' tips can also be held in the opposite direction, but never across the tips of the fur.) You might find that it is easier to trim the bear's head after the features are on but before it is attached to the body. The advantage of trimming it at this stage is that you can easily turn and hold the head from any angle. You can also easily trim around areas that would be difficult to reach if the head was on the body, such as under the chin.

Trimming can be a daunting process when you first start making bears, but it can quickly become one of the most enjoyable parts of the process. If at first you are unsure what to trim, or think "if I take off too much it won't grow back!" take a hard look at your bear's head.

Can you see his eyes clearly or are they lost in the fur? If the eyes need clearing they will only need it around the inner third of the eye as the fur should be "growing" away from the outside edge. This is one of the few times you will need to use the points of the scissors. Dig the points gently into the inner curve of the eye and trim away any fur that obscures it, as in *Fig. 65A*.

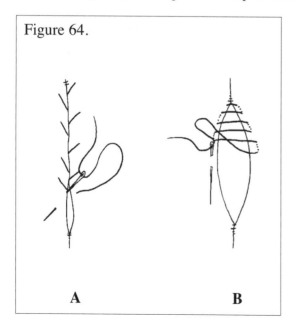

Figure 64.

A   B

Look at the head from front on; does the fur that runs from the outer edges of the nose up the gusset seams obscure the eyes? The inner corner of the eyes may now be clear but the fur down the length of the muzzle may still be in the way. It may be necessary to trim away the fur at an angle to help shape the top edges of the muzzle, as well as to clear the path from the nose to the eyes, as in *Fig. 65B*.

Now look at his mouth; can it be seen or is it completely hidden by the fur? If it is hidden, use your fingers to smooth it back and see whether trimming would show a smiling or a stern mouth. If he is smiling under his fur you might choose to expose it. If he is not a very happy bear the way you trim the fur around the mouth can improve his expression. The fur need not be trimmed away completely, but angling the cut from shorter at the base of the septum stitch to longer at the edges of the smile (as in *Fig. 66A*) will give you a nice natural look and expose the inner half of the mouth. Only exposing the start of the mouth can also conceal a rather sour or even slightly crooked expression. You can follow along the mouth line all the way to fully expose the smile.

Similarly, have a look at his chin from the front and the side. If your bear is supposed to be a female then a beard may not be appropriate. Try graduating the cut back (as in *Fig. 66B*) from short at the inverted V of the mouth back to the fur's full length, either under the chin or all the way back to the neck.

For a natural look on the muzzle, try graduating the fur from fairly short around the nose and mouth to its full length by the time it reaches the base of the muzzle at the eyes. If you look at your dog or cat you will see that the fur is short and velvet-like at the mouth and nose. To graduate the fur, always hold the points of the scissors further away from the fur than the base of the blades. This will ensure that as you snip with your scissors angled like this (and in the direction of the nap of the fur) you will not be chopping into the fur but layering it.

If you have sewn on the ears and one ear looks slightly larger than the other, or perhaps both ears are a little bigger than you would like, the ears can also be trimmed down. (They can of course be removed, re-edged and sewn back on, but sometimes the difference in size is small enough to be corrected by trimming.) If you want to trim down an ear, it is important to make the finished ear look as natural as possible. The first cutting will involve a "hard edge" as you cut around the curve of the ear as in *Fig. 67A*. Then feather the inner edges of the ear at an angle as in *Fig. 68A*, followed by the outer edges (*Fig. 68B*), and finally soften the whole curve by taking tiny snips with the points of the scissors all along the rim as in *Fig. 68C*.

The finished result should blend in perfectly with the fur on the head. If only one ear needs a little trimming to match it to the other one, the small difference in the length of the fur between the two ears will not be noticeable.

Trimming can also be done on other parts of the body. You might like a worn look to the paws and choose to trim back the edges of the fur around the paw and foot pads. If you are working on "antiquing" your bear, look at how old bears wear with time. The outer edges of the ears, the tummies, the muzzles and foreheads and parts of the arms tend to lose their fur and get worn and grubby as they age with love.

Figure 65.

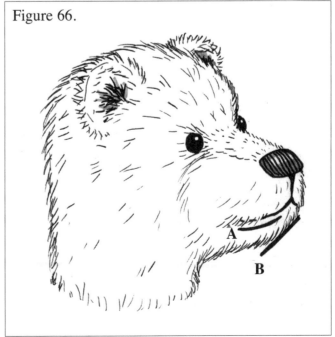

Figure 66.

Some bear makers who specialize in old-look teddies even "age" the mohair before they use it by staining, cutting, patch-dying, tie-dying, distressing, scrubbing, even tumbling it with stones in a cement mixer!

Coloring, painting, and **airbrushing** can also be used to add extra detail to your finished bear. Paints, powder pigments, inks, and dyes can all be used for special effects and to give added life to your creation. Brushes, sea sponges, sponge tipped applicators and airbrushes are all good for different painted effects. Look at the colors of the fur on real bears and other animals to get ideas for natural styles, or use your imagination for fantasy colors.

There is no reason why the painted effects have to be limited to the finished bear. Why not paint the mohair fabric before use, either on the backing or the fur side. You can even experiment with hand-tipping your mohair in unusual color combinations.

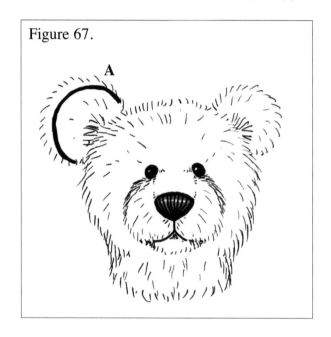

Figure 67.

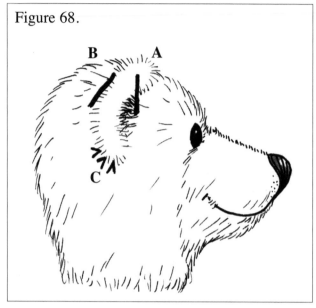

Figure 68.

SPARES

Extra pieces of fur left over from making the bear can be stuffed inside the body of the bear to be used for patches when the bear wears out. This information should be included on the bear's swing tag. Similarly, you might think of including an extra eye, with sewing instructions, in a little scrap fabric bag placed inside the body.

Alternatively you can think of the bear's body as a time capsule, especially if the bear is commissioned. The person who has ordered the bear might like to have some special little object placed inside the bear, especially if it is going to be a future heirloom.

ACCESSORIES AND CLOTHING

Collecting interesting trims, fabrics, miniature toys, buttons and any other little treasures can be a hobby in itself, but it is especially satisfying when your finds can be put to good use in your creations.

Stockpiling such items is a characteristic of many bear makers, whether it is merely with ribbons or with a whole range of interesting objects. All your treasures will come in handy sometime and could save you delays when you have to go out and source for that perfect finishing touch.

Having a stock of accessories on hand can also inspire a whole new line of bears, so take them out from time to time and play with them. Arranging them in color groups, for example, ribbons with buttons, feathers, fabrics, berries, beads and cord, can also help the imagination. When designing clothes try using paper towels as they can be molded to fit more easily than tissue. If planning on making a hat for your bear, the hat can be kept in shape by building up the head underneath, or perhaps omitting one ear so that the hat sits well on the head.

This is a 12in (30cm) bear with a built-on suit of clothes. When making a bear in this style it is a good idea to use short pile mohair so that there is not too much of a difference in size between the furry and the "clothed" parts of the bear. If you use long pile mohair the bear will tend to look skinned rather than as though it is wearing clothes. It may also be necessary to plump up the parts of the bear that will be "clothed" in order to balance out the overall look.

This style of bear can be made up in many different forms, depending on what type of outfit you want to make. The "clothes" could be also made of colored mohair rather than ultrasuede or fabric, and they could also reach the wrists and ankles rather than the knees and elbows. The feet could be made as slippers or with boots or shoes. The outfit could range from pajamas to jockey's silks. Use your imagination to adapt this pattern into your style of bear.

When marking out the pattern the inner and outer arm and leg pieces are identical so remember to only mark one left and one right joint mark on each pair of limbs. If spots are marked on all the pieces there is a chance that the ink may bleed through to the right side, and also a chance that holes will be pierced for jointing on two lefts or two rights instead of a pair of limbs.

When making up the pattern first sew up the pieces that have been cut into sections, for example the paws to the arms, the bottoms of the legs to the tops, and the bottom half of the body to the top half. The arms, legs and bodies can then be sewn together as normal.

After sewing, turn and joint the limbs to the body, using either the lock nuts as specified in the materials list or heavy cotter pins. Complete the head, stuff and close all seams. (Details for making up the bear are to be found in the Construction section.) When the bear is finished the trim can be added to the "clothes" to complete the costume. Ribbons cut into strips slightly longer than the waist to knee measurement are stitched on around the waistband and the knees. This extra length will allow the ribbon to balloon out and create the look of pantaloons. Different ribbon is then sewn over the wrists, waistband and knees to edge the costume, with further lace or trim at the wrists and knees if desired. A wide band of pleated silk was folded in half and tied around the neck with a narrow cord, producing the ruff collar. A lace collar would also look good with this outfit.

Using fine beading thread, seed beads and a thin beading needle,

the bodice and sleeves can be beaded. In this case three beads were used on each spot, blending in gold and green beads together. The position of the beads were measured and marked out on the body prior to the sewing to create a pattern.

The hat is made up by sewing A (the crown) to B (the sides) to C (the brim). Sew A to B first inside out, then turn it through and sew the beret shape to the brim from the inside. If you want the brim to be stiffer you can either iron on stiffening to the underside or add a layer of cardboard (cut slightly smaller then the brim) and then cover it with another layer of ultrasuede. If you do use a double layer for the brim you might want to cover the raw edge with a narrow cord or some other trim. The crown of the hat could also look good if it was beaded to match the bodice. The hat is finished by adorning it with ribbons and feathers. It is easy to dye feathers to match the outfit, either by using fabric dyes, marking pens or food dyes.

As a final detail for the little Laughing Cavalier, the bear's face has been trimmed to give him a long moustache, which was then darkened with a marking pen and stiffened and shaped with hair gel into a "waxed moustache".

A DRESSED BEAR

Materials

A "fat" 1/8 yard (.12 meter) of mohair, 3/8in (2cm) pile in golden tan.

12in (30cm) x 18in (46cm) of ultrasuede in bottle green.

12in (30cm) x 18in (46cm) of ultrasuede in golden tan.

6in (15cm) x 8in (20cm) of beige wool felt.

1 pair of 9mm boot button eyes.

10 — 1-3/4in (45mm) discs with 1/4" (7mm) ID (internal diameter).

10 — 3/4in (45mm) washers with 1/4" (7mm) ID (internal diameter).

5 — 1/4in (7mm) by 1" (2.5cm) long hexagonal headed bolts.

4 — 1/4in (7mm) nylock or lock nuts.

1 — 1/4in (7mm) ordinary hex nut.

(Or five cotter pins instead of the above nuts and bolts.)

DMC #5 thread for nose and claws.

Polyfill stuffing.

Assorted ribbons, lace, trim, feathers and beads.

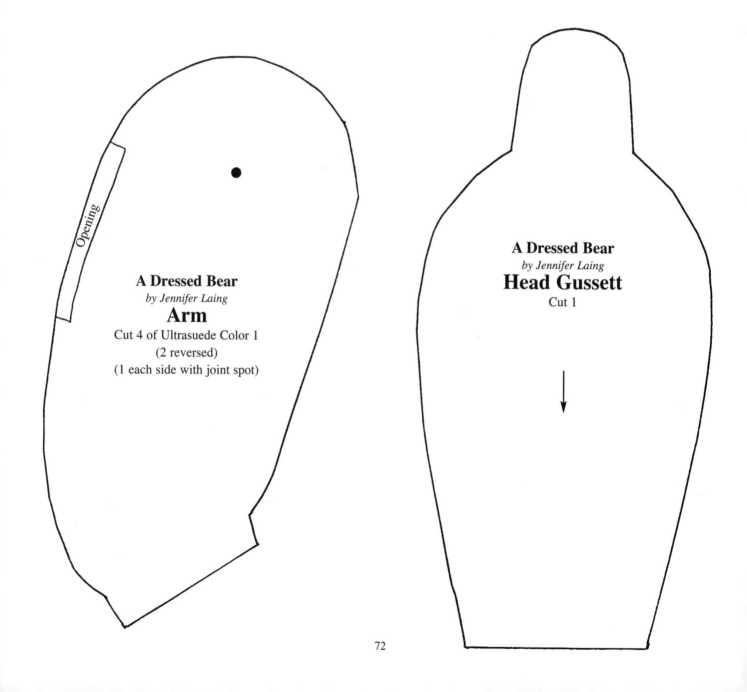

A Dressed Bear
by Jennifer Laing
Arm
Cut 4 of Ultrasuede Color 1
(2 reversed)
(1 each side with joint spot)

A Dressed Bear
by Jennifer Laing
Head Gussett
Cut 1

Opening

A DRESSED BEAR

A Dressed Bear
by Jennifer Laing
Ear
Cut 4 of Mohair

A Dressed Bear
by Jennifer Laing
Head
Cut 2 (1 reversed) of Mohair

Opening

A Dressed Bear
by Jennifer Laing
Top of Leg
Cut 4 (2 reversed) of
Ultrasuede Color 2

A Dressed Bear
by Jennifer Laing
Bottom of Legs
Cut 4 (2 reversed) of Mohair

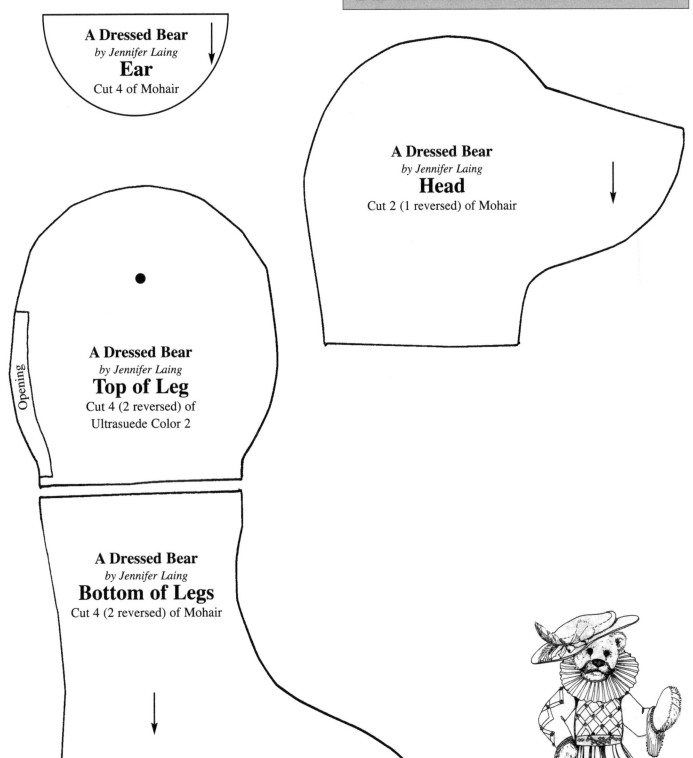

A DRESSED BEAR

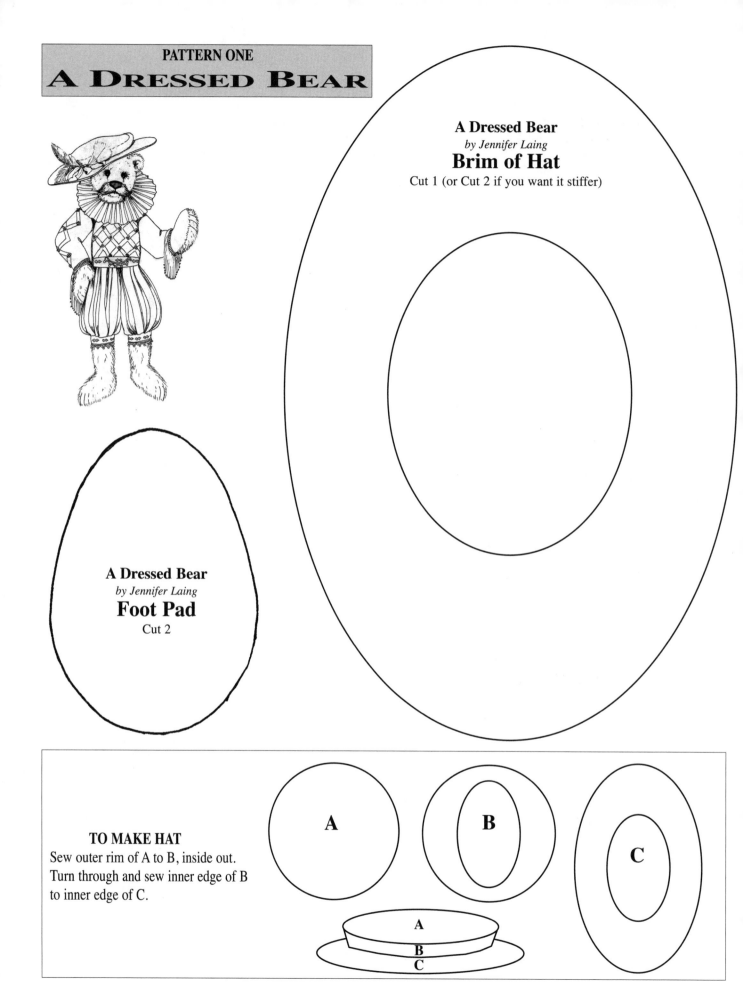

A Dressed Bear
by Jennifer Laing
Brim of Hat
Cut 1 (or Cut 2 if you want it stiffer)

A Dressed Bear
by Jennifer Laing
Foot Pad
Cut 2

A

B

C

TO MAKE HAT
Sew outer rim of A to B, inside out.
Turn through and sew inner edge of B
to inner edge of C.

A
B
C

A Dressed Bear
by Jennifer Laing

Crown Rim
Cut 1

A Dressed Bear
by Jennifer Laing
Paw
Cut 2 of mohair (1 reversed)
Cut 2 of felt (1 reversed)

A Dressed Bear
by Jennifer Laing
Crown
Cut 1

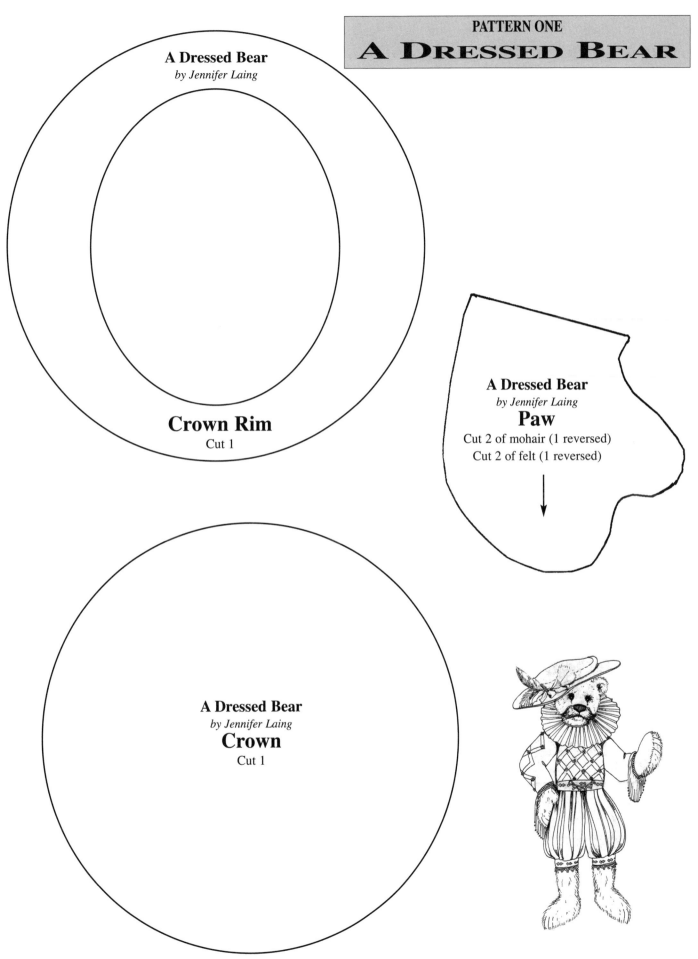

A DRESSED BEAR

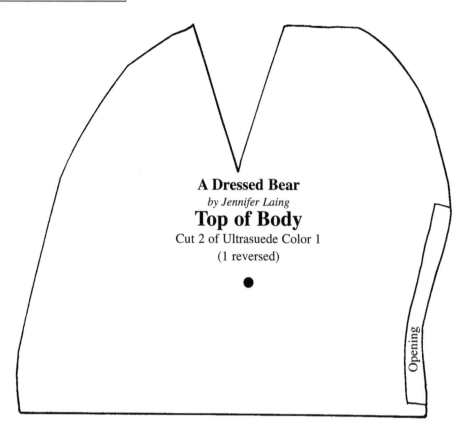

A Dressed Bear
by Jennifer Laing
Top of Body
Cut 2 of Ultrasuede Color 1
(1 reversed)

●

Opening

A Dressed Bear
by Jennifer Laing
Top of Body
Cut 2 of Ultrasuede Color 2
(1 reversed)

●

This is a 10in (25cm) bear with big paws and a bad posture! His head is angled forward slightly, making him sit in a slumped position and giving him some extra "attitude" and he has a little tail. He is made of two colors of mohair. The inset tummy and muzzle, and lining of his ears are in the second lighter color. The legs are straight while the arms are slightly bent, and the arms contain Flexlimb for added movement. Soft stuffing or pellet/polyfill stuffing would suit this bear. If you want to use pellets, then confine their use to the body if you are also using Flexlimb in the arms.

This pattern can also be made up in a number of ways. Instead of having a brown bear with a blond tummy he could be a black bear with a brown chest, or a polar bear with a gray muzzle and inner ears. Tipped mohair would also work very well with this style of bear. Experiment with the length of the mohair too, as a certain shagginess could add some extra character to your bear. (Just remember that if you use a long mohair you will need to "carve out" the face more in order to reveal its expression and to bring the fur into proportion on the head. The fur on the ears could be left in the natural longer state or they could also be trimmed down.)

As with the Pattern One bear, the pieces of the pattern that have been cut into sections need to be sewn together first and then the bear can be made up as normal. As you are using different colors you will need to use the appropriate colore thread for the parts you are sewing. You can also blur the distinct line between the two colors of fur by painting on an intermediate color at the join. The lining of the ears can also be given an extra depth in this way. Permanent marking pens are good for this if you do not have an airbrush, and will blend in the two colors in a natural looking way.

The paws can be left plain or be given paw pads and toes. In this case the bear has appliquéd paw pads of suede on ultrasuede, but why not just paint the pads on instead? You can also add details to appliquéd pads by either painting an extra dimension to them or by adding padding underneath. Padding can be either polyfill stuffing or an extra layer of suede which is slightly smaller than the appliqué.

The tail is added on after the bear has been completed. It is important that the position of the tail does not interfere with his sitting down, so seat the bear first to determine the right place for it. The tail can be sewn on empty like an ear, or it can be softly stuffed to give it some body. Rather than sewing the tail on flat, try sewing the edges on in an oval shape to give it a more natural appearance.

The nose has been lightly coated with melted beeswax after embroidery, then buffed with a sheet of paper to give it a smooth shiny finish. The wax will slightly darken the color of the thread used on the nose. You can also paint additional shading on the nose prior to waxing. Why not give him nostrils?

PATTERN TWO
A WILD BEAR CUB

Materials:

A "fat" 1/4 yard (.23 meter) of 1/2in (1cm) pile brown mohair.
A "fat" 1/8 yard (.12 meter) of 1/2in (1cm) pile blonde mohair.
6in x 8in (15cm x 20cm) of sand ultrasuede.
6in x 8in (15cm x 20cm) of brown suede.
1 pair of 10mm painted back glass eyes.
10 — 1-1/2in discs (40mm) with a 1/4in (7mm) ID (internal diameter).
10 — 3/4in (20mm) washers with a 1/4in (7mm) ID (internal diameter).
5 — 1/4 in (7mm) hexagonal headed bolts x 1in (2.5cm) long.
4 — 1/4in (7mm) nylock or lock nuts.
1 — 1/4in (7mm) ordinary hex nut.
(Or five cotter pins instead of the above nuts and bolts.)
2 — Flexlimb pieces, cut to fit the length of the arms. Polyfill and pellet stuffing.
DMC #5 thread for nose and claws.
Permanent ink felt marking pens for painted details.

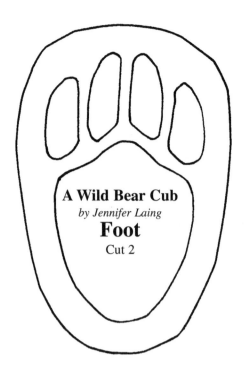

A Wild Bear Cub
by Jennifer Laing
Foot
Cut 2

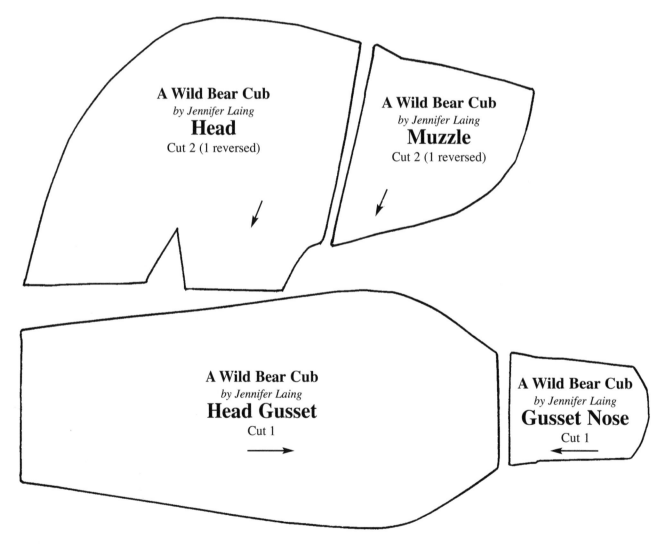

A Wild Bear Cub
by Jennifer Laing
Head
Cut 2 (1 reversed)

A Wild Bear Cub
by Jennifer Laing
Muzzle
Cut 2 (1 reversed)

A Wild Bear Cub
by Jennifer Laing
Head Gusset
Cut 1

A Wild Bear Cub
by Jennifer Laing
Gusset Nose
Cut 1

A WILD BEAR CUB

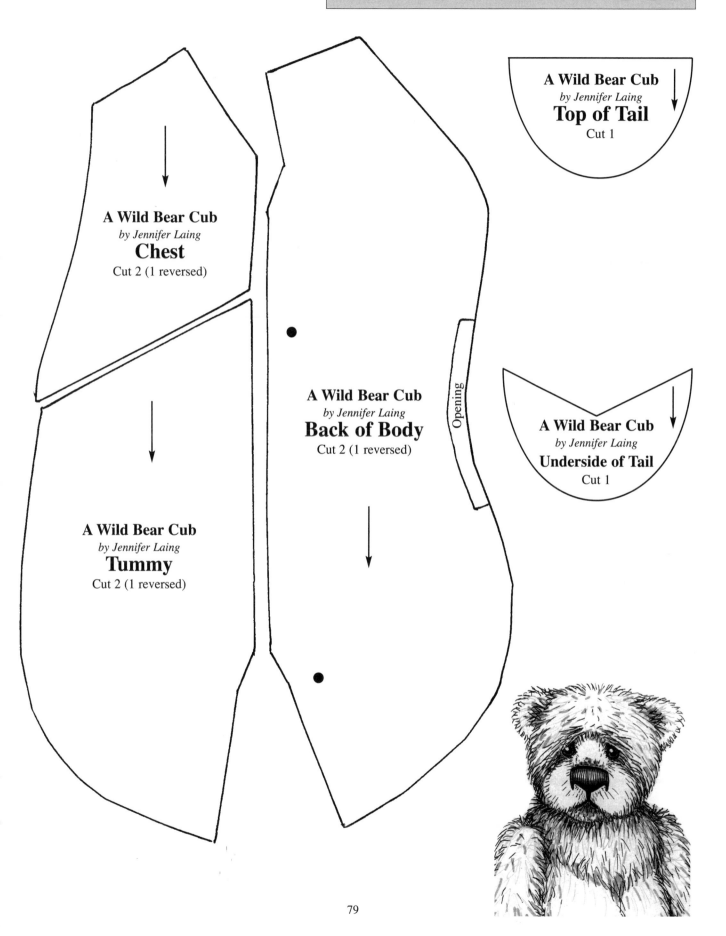

A Wild Bear Cub
by Jennifer Laing
Chest
Cut 2 (1 reversed)

A Wild Bear Cub
by Jennifer Laing
Tummy
Cut 2 (1 reversed)

A Wild Bear Cub
by Jennifer Laing
Back of Body
Cut 2 (1 reversed)

Opening

A Wild Bear Cub
by Jennifer Laing
Top of Tail
Cut 1

A Wild Bear Cub
by Jennifer Laing
Underside of Tail
Cut 1

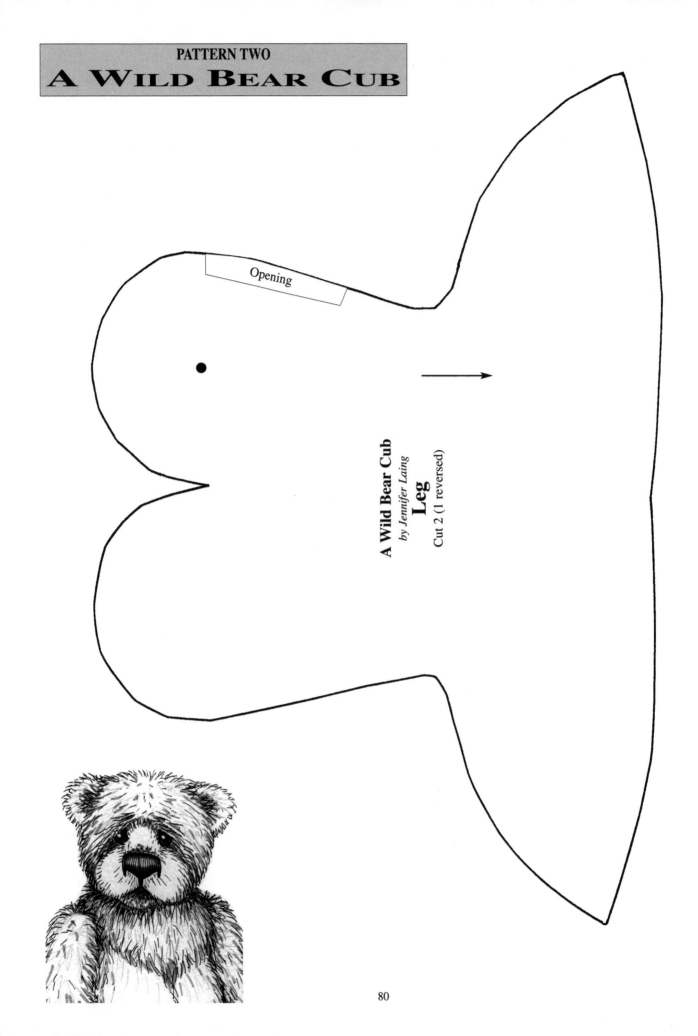

PATTERN TWO
A WILD BEAR CUB

Opening

A Wild Bear Cub
by Jennifer Laing
Leg
Cut 2 (1 reversed)

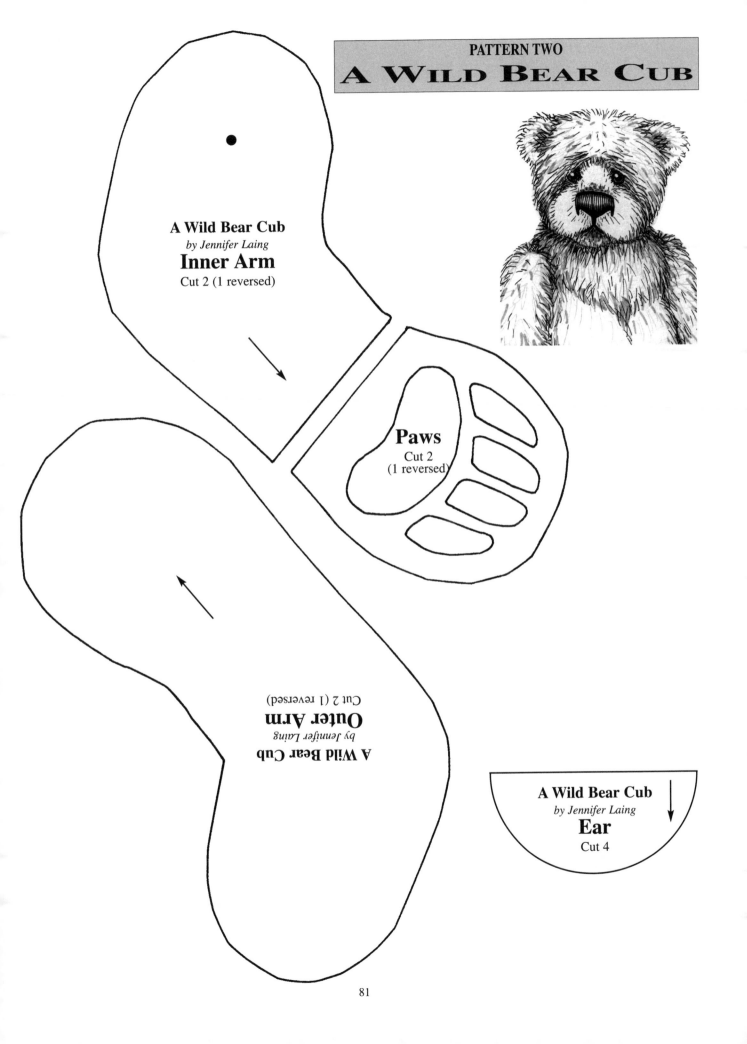

A Wild Bear Cub
by Jennifer Laing
Inner Arm
Cut 2 (1 reversed)

Paws
Cut 2
(1 reversed)

Cut 2 (1 reversed)
Outer Arm
by Jennifer Laing
A Wild Bear Cub

A Wild Bear Cub
by Jennifer Laing
Ear
Cut 4

A FOUR LEGGED BEAR

This style of bear was invented before the turn of the century, and before the jointed teddy bear came into existence. Pull toys were very popular and many animals on wheels were designed. This pattern has a bit of a contemporary twist, as it has a jointed neck and jointed legs which give it extra life and movement. He is 16-inches (46cm) long and stands 10-inches (25 cm) high.

If you wanted to, you could easily make it a bear on wheels, making the framework and wheels of metal or wood, or whatever you have at hand. The feet could be fixed to the framework or base by using Velcro, stud fasteners, bolts or wire down through the legs from the joints, depending on how permanently you want him attached to the wheels. A pull chain or lead could be attached to either the front of the wheels, or to the bear by having a collar and lead on him.

He is made of tipped mohair but try using different styles of mohair to see what effects you can achieve. The body is in three pieces with a tummy gusset. There are two discs cut out of mohair which are sewn into the neck openings on the head and on the body before the head is attached to the body. This means that the neck is not gathered in around the joint disc and it gives a smooth line from the head to the body.

His nose is made of leather (there is a template in the pattern for it) and stitched in place with the ends of the T-shape pulled down to form nostrils. The leather is stitched to the muzzle with ladder stitch all the way around the edge. His septum line and mouth are embroidered with DMC no. 5 in a shade that matches the leather.

His legs could easily be changed around, and he could have "teddy bear arms" if you wanted. The shape of his paw pads can also be varied, and extra detailing such as toes or leather claws could easily be applied.

A FOUR LEGGED BEAR

Materials

A "fat" 1/3 yd. (.3 meter) of tipped mohair 3/4in (2cm) long.

6in (15 cm) square of felt or ultrasuede for paw pads.

1 pair of 10mm eyes.

10 — 2-1/2in (65mm) discs with 1/4in (7mm) ID (internal diameter).

10 washers with 1/4in (7mm) ID (internal diameter).

5 — 1/4in (7mm) hex bolts, 1in (3cm) long (or substitute 5 strong cotter pins.)

4 — 1/4in (7mm) hex lock nuts.

1 — 1/4in (7mm) ordinary hex nut.

Polyfill stuffing.

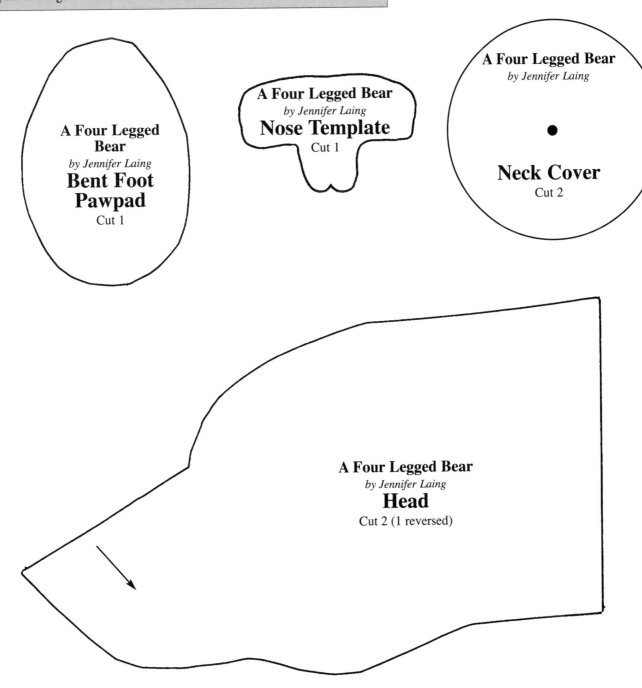

A Four Legged Bear
by Jennifer Laing
Bent Foot Pawpad
Cut 1

A Four Legged Bear
by Jennifer Laing
Nose Template
Cut 1

A Four Legged Bear
by Jennifer Laing

Neck Cover
Cut 2

A Four Legged Bear
by Jennifer Laing
Head
Cut 2 (1 reversed)

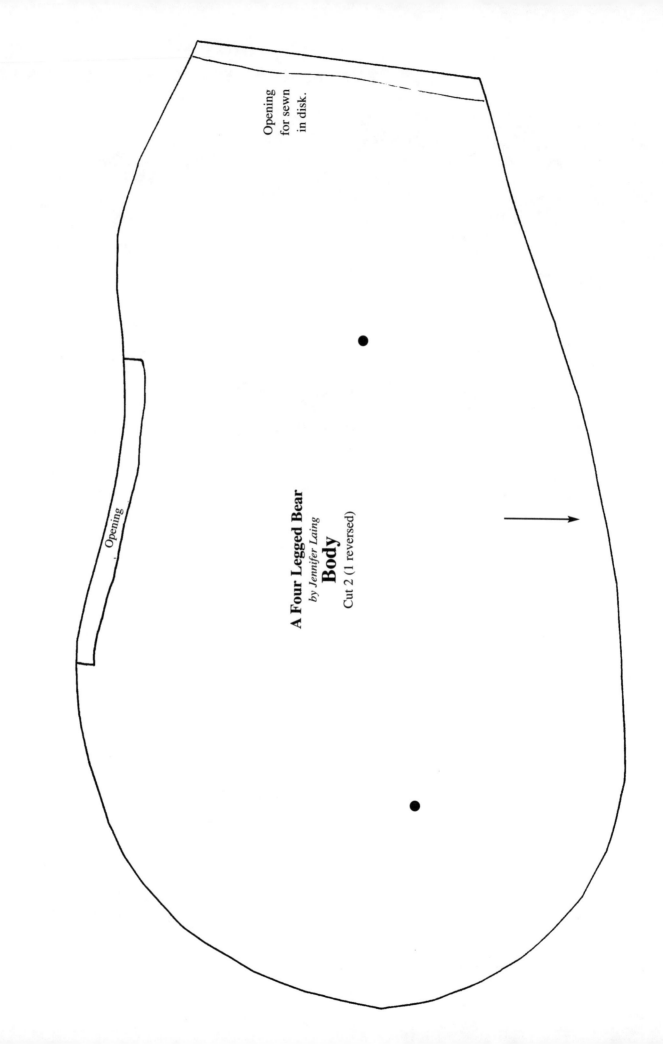

Opening for sewn in disk.

Opening

A Four Legged Bear
by Jennifer Laing
Body
Cut 2 (1 reversed)

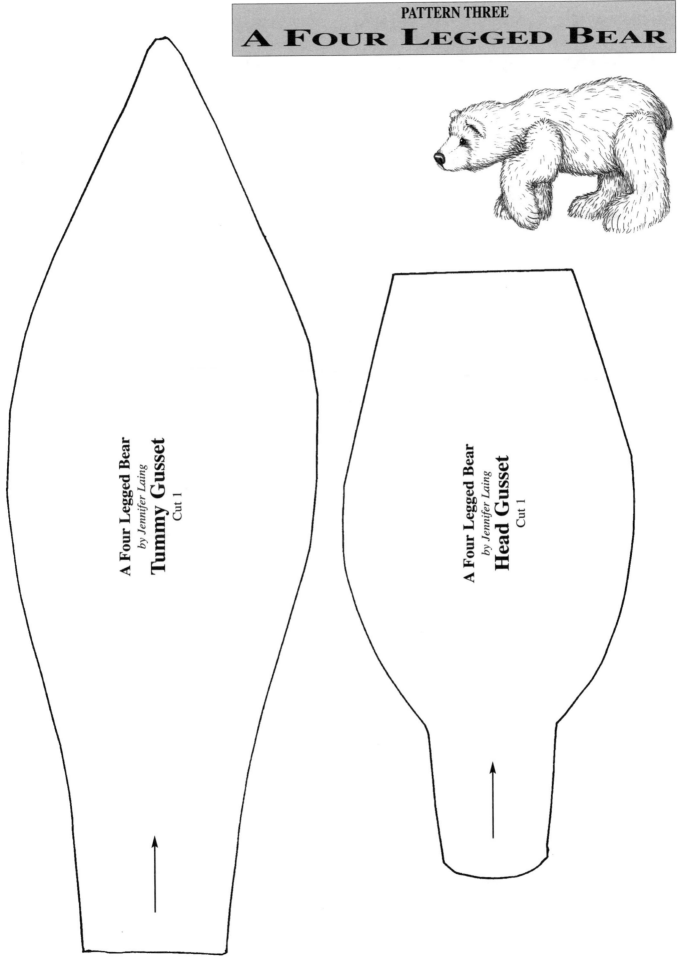

A Four Legged Bear
by Jennifer Laing
Tummy Gusset
Cut 1

A Four Legged Bear
by Jennifer Laing
Head Gusset
Cut 1

A Four Legged Bear

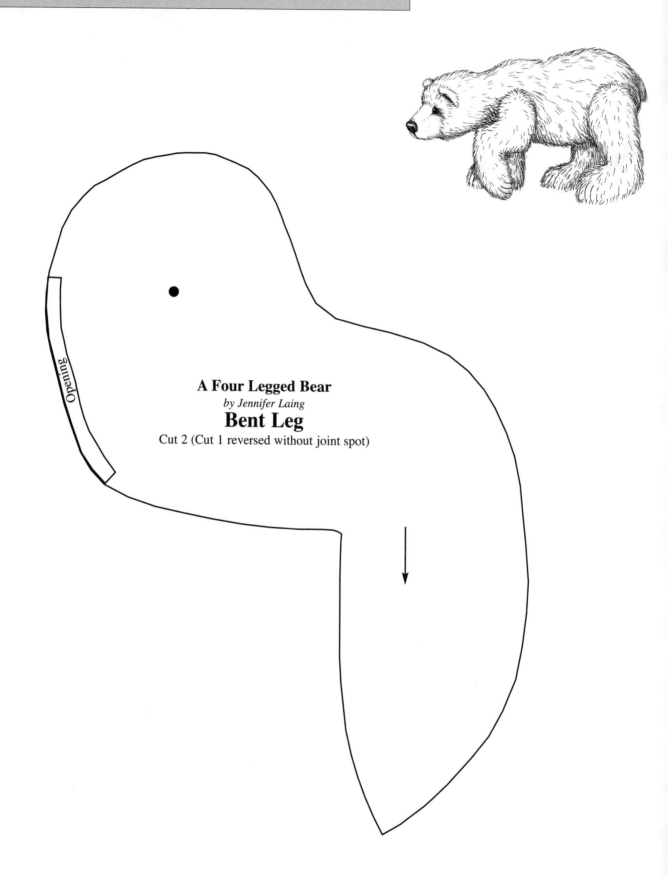

A Four Legged Bear
by Jennifer Laing
Bent Leg
Cut 2 (Cut 1 reversed without joint spot)

Opening

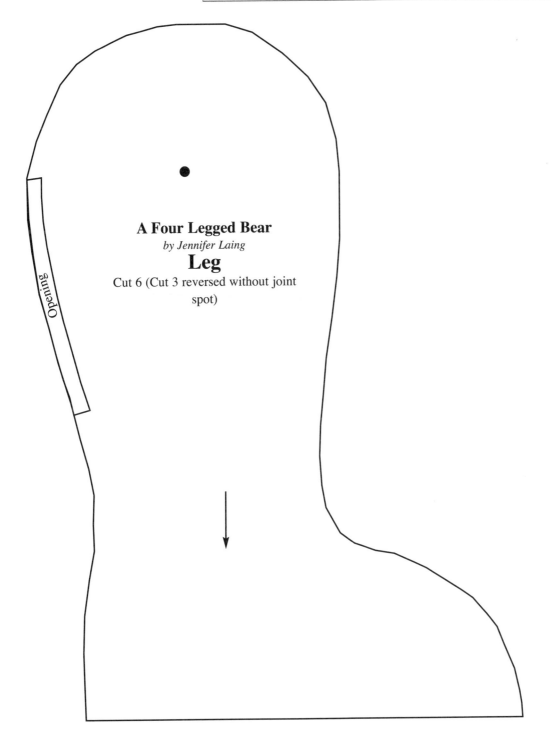

A Four Legged Bear
by Jennifer Laing
Leg
Cut 6 (Cut 3 reversed without joint spot)

Opening

A FOUR LEGGED BEAR

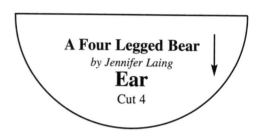

A Four Legged Bear
by Jennifer Laing
Top Side of Tail
Cut 1

A Four Legged Bear
by Jennifer Laing
Ear
Cut 4

A Four Legged Bear
by Jennifer Laing
Foot
Pawpad
Cut 3

A Four Legged Bear
by Jennifer Laing
Bottom Side of Tail
Cut 1

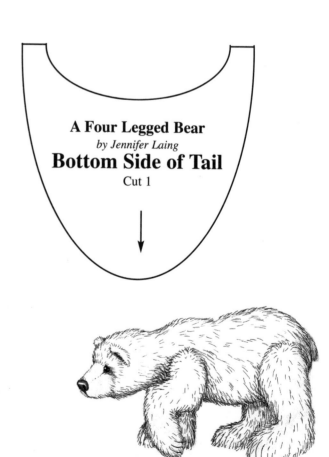

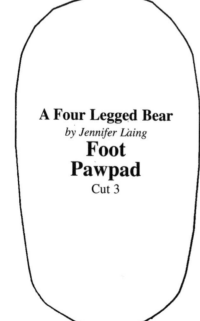

RUNNING YOUR OWN BEAR BUSINESS

Is it for you?

There are many reasons for wanting to run your own business, especially if you are frustrated with your present career and want more creative freedom. If you are to succeed, however, you need more than just dreams, you need firm plans and initiative, skill, talent and perseverance. The worldwide artist bear market is now very competitive, so you need to be confident that you have something new and special to offer. It is a sobering thought that statistically over 80% of small businesses fail within their first two years of operation, so before you give up your day job think about your goals, your plans, your motivation and your financial resources.

In order to run your own business you will need to be highly motivated, self-reliant, decisive, disciplined, dedicated, well-organized, responsible, professional and prepared to work long hours by yourself.

Can you handle isolation and overcome distractions? You will need to have the space at home or else you will have to rent a separate studio (which will mean extra overhead to be covered). Your home business will affect your family and even your pets, so think about whether you can cope with it. You need to be able to handle stress well (don't think that you will be having a less stressful environment if you run your own business) as well as being a good time manager.

Do you know the market?

Also think about whether you really know the business. Loving bears and collecting them is one thing, but do you know the bear business and the market? Do you know how to deal professionally at shows, with galleries, retail outlets or agents? Proper marketing is about having the right bear for the right market. Appeal is important but so is quality and a suitable price.

Doing Your Business Homework

If you feel confident after considering all these facts you can get down to basics and find out if you can afford to do it by **assessing your personal worth**. This is done by calculating your **assets** (what you own) – **liabilities** (what you owe).

You also need to prepare a detailed **cash flow budget** for twelve months, estimating how much you expect to receive and to pay out in the year. Even if you have not made bears for a full year you can calculate how many bears you can comfortably make in a week and multiply it up to a year, allowing for holidays and time off for sickness. The cost of materials in bear making is high, particularly when using mohair and other expensive fabrics such as pure wool felt and ultrasuede. You will also have large advertising expenses, as well as travel expenses if you intend to sell at shows.

It can be a good idea to use the services of an **accountant** or **financial planner** at this stage, and you can also see if your local Small Business Center can advise you. Even banks can have helpful guides and brochures on setting up a business. Find a professional accountant with knowledge of the needs of artists and craftspeople to assist you with your tax.

Income protection **insurance** should be considered, and if you plan to go into business with a partner you should have a partnership agreement and perhaps partnership insurance. Be aware, however, that business partnerships can be difficult and demanding relationships.

Setting Up

Opening a separate **business account** at your bank is important, in order to keep your business transactions separate from your personal ones. Facilities for accepting credit card sales are recommended as they can help to generate sales. A **post office** box is also a good idea for all your business mail as it helps maintain your privacy and security.

You will need to **register your business** name with the State office of Corporate Affairs or its equivalent. Most craftspeople spend all their business lives as **sole traders** (or proprietors), but should your business expand you may have a partnership or even a **proprietary company**. A sole trader or proprietor is the cheapest and simplest form of business structure, but you are liable for provisional tax as well as taxation as an individual. As a sole trader your profitability depends upon your actions and your health. Your Taxation Office may have a small business kit or guide for you containing a business name registration form and information on taxation responsibilities as a small business.

Contact your business License or Information Center to see whether you will need approval for conducting your business from your home. Municipalities and councils have very different regulations and application procedures governing home-based business.

Financing Your Business

It is important to have your finances in order so that you can maintain a business, and ideally your own savings should be enough to start your business. If you need a loan to get it off the ground you can get one supplied by a bank or a finance company, and it can be short-term, medium-term or long-term. If borrowing, however, never use short-term funds for long-term projects or vice versa as this is too expensive and wasteful.

The Business Plan

If you need to borrow funds for your business then you will need to be able to present the bank or finance company with a business plan. A business plan is a good idea in any event as it is a guide to your business and shows where you hope to go with it. Your Business Plan should contain the following:

Cover sheet – showing name, business name, address, contact numbers.
Contents of the business plan – purpose of the business, aims.
Business history – including resume.
Products and productions.
Your market.
Sales and marketing.
Staffing plans.
Financial information.
Sources and applications for funding.

Equipment list.
Past performance – tax returns, balance sheets.
Break even analysis – future projections.
Sales and gross margins.
Expenses.
Cash flow budget over 12 months.
Appendices, including references, contracts, etc.

The Presentation Package

Promotion is communication. The idea is to educate the market and get your name known. Your creations will not sell themselves without it, so you need a professional image. Your personal style should be communicated by the coordinated use of your personal presentation, visual images and language. This can take time and money but it is an important consideration and an important investment in your business.

You will need an image, logo, text and colors that are as individual as you are and that say what you want them to say. It is important to have a logo that is uniquely yours, so don't be tempted to use a commercially available rubber teddy bear stamp. When people see the stamp they won't think *of your* bears, they will think of where they last saw that stamp used which is undoubtedly on something other than your work. If the logo is your design and depicts what could only be one of your bears, then your logo will become recognized as a symbol of you and your work. It need not be fancy, in fact the simpler the better. (Think of those golden arches - a simple logo immediately recognized around the world!) If you cannot draw or design your own logo, approach a graphic designer who understands what you want to express.

Keep your design simple and keep the stationery standard in size to avoid extra costs in mailing and printing. Avoid ornate typefaces or all capitals and don't use too many typefaces together. Get several printing quotes and costs on different sized print runs. Use color selectively as the cost can blow out your printing budget. Other special effects which can look great but can also cost a lot more include die-cutting, foil stamping, embossing and debossing.

For your business you will need to have printed your logo letterhead, as well as business cards, invoices, receipts, order forms, credit notes, packing slips and With Compliments slips. You will also need swing tags, labels, brochures and catalogues, show display kit, signage, publicity blurb, portfolio and advertising material. This might be too much to start off with so just get the most important things first, which would definitely include business cards, catalogues and swing tags. You can add to your range as you progress, but keep to the image you have established.

When printing your brochure or catalogue, you want it to have a long life so include your price list and photos as a separate section which can be updated when needed. Get your photographs taken professionally. Keep the catalogue readable and professional and continue the use of your logo, type styles and paper. If you are thinking of the international market then be aware you might need some foreign language translations. As the printing and mailing of your catalogue can be an ongoing expense, think about charging a nominal fee for them in order to help cover costs.

Marketing

The 4 P's of marketing are Product, Price, Place, and Promotion. Think about what it is you are selling, how much people will pay, where and how you will sell it and how you will present it. Research your market through its specialist books, journals and magazines, attend shows and specialist stores, ask questions. If you intend to make a soft toy rather than an adult collectable then your market will be very different. Soft toys have a more mass market appeal and your price structure and turnover will reflect that. Artist bears are definitely a luxury item, therefore the market will be smaller and more specialized. Look at your particular market and analyze your strengths, weaknesses, opportunities and threats. See if there is a vacant niche in the market that you can fill with your creations.

Be prepared to constantly appraise your own range of work and to move on to new things. Keep abreast of current trends and styles in your chosen field. Your customers' tastes will change and so should yours. A trademark style can help identify you but do not let it become stale. Competitors will always be around to copy good ideas, so be a leader not a follower.

Pricing

Pricing plays an important part of the successful marketing of your work, and it is not such a simple thing to do in the arts and crafts. You will need to establish your costs first, but you will also need to consider the competition as well as the influence of supply and demand. You should also think about whether you are aiming at a high profit one-off sale or at repeat business.

If you enter the market by underselling you might seem successful initially, but are you selling because the quality and appeal is really good or because the prices are really low? You might end up literally selling yourself short if you continue to undersell. Similarly, one cannot expect to start selling with prices equal to those of the biggest names in the market. As an unknown you will have build up your reputation for style, quality and originality and this takes time.

You will need to establish how many hours it takes you to make one bear, and how many bears you can comfortably make in a week. Material costs and labor hours should give you a wholesale or minimum cost price. You will need to add sales tax where applicable and your retail margin (often around 33%) to give you a retail price. Will this output give you the required income you need? If this is a hobby or part-time career then it may not be so crucial but if you intend to rely on it for an income then it is important to work this out.

Retail and Wholesale

Where do you intend to sell? This can depend on your personality and on your location. It can also depend on your output. If you hand sew your bears for example, and only make a few a year, it may not be worth your time or money to wholesale. If you have a good output, can afford to sell wholesale and want to get your stock and your name promoted more widely, then wholesale may be for you.

Wholesale can be through specialist bear shops, gift outlets, arts and crafts stores, even department stores and art galleries. You need to look at your annual output and see where it will best be distributed. Do you want to sell locally, nationally or internationally? If you only sell in one location, you could be missing better exposure opportunities. Selling too widely, on the other hand, can mean that you might take on more than you can handle.

Once again, it is important to do your homework. Find out your favorite bear shops, whether in your area or around the world. Visit them if at all possible, or find out what they are like and how well they are run. (It can be very hard to tell what a retailer is like from only their advertising. What may seem to be a huge specialist bear shop judging from the size and style of the advertisements may in fact be a warehouse which sells by mail order or a mediocre gift shop with a small teddy bear corner.)

Make sure that they sell quality items and have the image you want. The best specialist stores will have very good reputations and are run by people who not only understand the business but love bears and are experienced in doing business with individuals like yourself.

If you have been advertising (see publicity section, page 92) then more than likely these stores will approach you. Once again, know what you can handle with your work load before agreeing to supply your work to anyone and build up a business relationship with the outlet involved. If corresponding by letter or fax, use your letterhead and send your brochure, resume and business card. Be professional and on time with your deliveries. Don't promise what you cannot deliver. Establish who is liable for freight costs and if possible get some form of contract, written agreement or invoice. If you are turned down, don't take it personally. The store knows its customers and their tastes and your work may just not be appropriate to that particular market.

If you are working with a good retail outlet you may find that they will go out of their way to help you promote your work. Not only might they give it prominent window or shelf display space (should you send additional signage) but they may sometimes advertise that they have your work for sale in specialist bear magazines or in their mail order catalogues. This is an excellent way of obtaining additional exposure at no cost to yourself. A good way of returning such a favor is to promise one-offs or exclusive limited editions for that store, so they are getting something special from you that no other retailer will have.

If you are selling on consignment to a retailer, make sure that you have a written agreement before you leave your goods with them. Work out whether they will be taking a commission on sales or whether they will be paying you your wholesale price. Make freight and insurance arrangements with them Also agree on the time frame and when you can either hear from them with your payment or collect your unsold stock. Make sure all goods are itemized and invoiced and that you both have copies.

Spend time on your packaging and packing and always make sure your goods are insured in transit. If sending your work internationally shop around for a courier or freight forwarding company who can put a deal together and take the worry out of it for you. They can also advise you on how to pack and correctly mark your boxes.

Sales Representatives

This is another way of selling your work, where you employ someone else to do the legwork for you. Sales representatives take your work to shops and shows and can arrange personal appearances for you. They work on a sales commission basis and often it can work out on a similar level as selling wholesale.

Shows & Mail-Order

Selling wholesale can often be more cost effective than direct selling, but direct selling has its own advantages. You can sell directly to the public from your studio or at craft fairs, specialist bear shows or even expos. You can also sell directly to customers by phone or mail order, paying by bank card, check or postal order arrangement.

If you are shy you might feel more comfortable to sell from home by mail order, through retail outlets, or have someone else sell your work at shows. There are some well-known names in this business who prefer to work this way and who are rarely seen. Although there may be no face-to-face contact with the customers, there is often a lot of correspondence which can build up into lasting friendships with collectors and fellow artists alike.

If you are only going to sell through mail order then your way of promoting yourself will rely on advertising. Merchant facilities (for a Mastercard/Visa business account for example) will give you a definite advantage and can help increase sales, but you should be aware of the additional costs involved in being able to offer this convenience (around 3-5%).

Taking part in shows and fairs not only gives you the opportunity to sell your work but also to educate and inform potential customers about the particular aspects of your work. It is also a great chance to meet the collectors and other artists, to get feedback on your work and to see what other artists are doing. There is always something to be learned from the professionals who have been in the business longer than you. Many great bear and display ideas are also to be found at shows, as well as the chance to buy from the suppliers. You will need to take along extra signage, business cards, brochures, order book, invoice book, merchant facilities, and items for your display. (A mobile phone is an excellent tool for getting on the spot approval for credit card transactions.)You are often required to provide your own table coverings, so think about your overall look and presentation.

It is important to make sure that attending shows is worth your time and money. It is not cost effective running all over the country to take part in every bear fair if your travel costs, accommodations, stand/stall price, lost work time and other outgoings outstrip your earnings from your sales. Once again, analyze your strategies and do your homework.

Publicity

You need to promote yourself in order to get your name known, to make your work more salable and to increase the public's knowledge of your particular contribution to the bear world, whatever that might be. If you have something newsworthy then you can easily get free publicity. Have you got a new item, a new technique or broken into a new export market? Send press releases and photographs to your local newspaper as well as to the national and international bear magazines. This form of publicity can be far-reaching as well as free.

Newspapers and magazines can also offer deals where if you take out advertising space with them you can get an editorial on you and your work. If the circulation and the cost of the advertising are worth it, this can be a good way of stretching your advertising dollars further.

Advertising is expensive but it can be a good way of getting your work seen around the world. Compare advertising rates and the circulation of the different specialist bear magazines. Don't limit yourself to your own local magazine if you can get better value advertising internationally. Make sure you have your photographs professionally taken and have the layout also done professionally if you do not have a computer at home. It can often be better value to take out a block booking of several issues to a single advertisement. If you do take a block booking, think about changing the photo in each issue, but keeping it within the same layout so that your logo will make a repeated impact while you increase public awareness of your range.

Use your advertising space to also announce your show schedule or store appearances for the year, and remember to use a business address or P.O. Box rather than your private address. If you do not do wholesale, mention that only retail inquiries are welcome in order to save correspondence costs replying to stores' inquiries.

Appearances can be a good way of promoting yourself and your work if you supply to shops. Specialist bear shops in particular are interested in having bear artists appear in their stores as this helps generate interest in the artists' work and generate extra sales. Work out the details with your retail outlet and perhaps time it with the release of your new work for sale in the store. Although you will not be paid to appear often your expenses can be covered by the organizer, or you can come to some arrangement. The organizer will also be advertising the event on your behalf so you and your work will be attracting further publicity.

Competitions and awards are another good way of getting publicity for the price of the entrance fee. If you are starting out in the business, competitions can be a good way of getting feedback from your peers, who will be judging the event and who will make comments and give advice on your critique sheet (if it is a good competition). Winning a competition or award can really help start you on your career path if you are a newcomer, or give your career a great boost if you have been at it for a while. International bear magazines often sponsor their own awards and they will give good coverage of the nominees and winners. It all helps to add to your reputation.

Networking is a major promotional tool, particularly in the artist bear business. If you attend shows regularly you will quickly build up a data base of clients, friends and associate artists. This network will help you discover which are the best shows to attend, the best stores to sell to, the nicest people to deal with. Your business potential can really expand through networking, and you can have a lot of fun and make a lot of friends along the way.

Don't just limit your sights to the local market, the international market is just as accessible through networking. If you don't want to travel the world to promote your bears, then you can do it from home on the Internet. There is a large and growing amount of information online on the teddy bear world, and many artists are successfully selling their bears all over the world via the net. It is also a great way to make friends with other collectors and catch up with all the latest business gossip.

Organization | *Your workspace*

is important, and although some of us are used to working in chaos a little organization never hurts. Start off by arranging your work schedule. Once you make a business out of your bears you will find that you often have your activities booked for a whole year ahead. Sit down and plan your year. Look at how many bears you will need to produce to fill all the orders and fill the tables at the shows you plan to attend. Make sure you have not taken on more than you are physically capable of doing. Note down the dates of deadlines required for things like auction pieces, limited editions for stores, one-off pieces for appearances, photographs or advertising copy. Ensure that you allow adequate time to order and purchase the materials you will need in order to make these bears and meet these deadlines.

Break down your work schedule into months and weeks and give yourself a list of what has to be done by the end of each week. Don't leave things till the last minute or you may find yourself sewing at two in the morning the day of a show in order to have some bears to put on the table. Not only will you be exhausted, you will quickly burn out by being unnecessarily hard on yourself.

Try cutting out your week's worth of bears in one day to minimize the mess and the vacuuming. Bag and label the pieces to avoid confusion. Keep a list of supplies as they start to run low, and don't run out of necessary items before you re-order them. If you have to make a limited edition, order all the mohair you will need in one order, otherwise you will have different dye lots and the fur can vary enormously in color. Similarly if you are hand-dyeing for an edition, do all the fur you will need at one time, otherwise you will never be able to match it.

Organize your supplies so they are easy to find and sort through. Mohair can be sorted according to color or length, but remember to tag those pieces you might be keeping for a special limited edition so you don't use them for something else. Keep your mohair dry and moth-free and if possible hang it rather than keeping it folded and stacked. Spools of ribbons can be kept on horizontal poles underneath shelves, and spools of threads can be kept in labeled drawers or hung on the wall on small wire bottle racks or spool holders. Joint discs and hardware can be kept in lidded buckets or tubs with the size printed on the lid. Eyes and small items like mini washers and tiny cotter pins are conveniently stored in stackable compartmentalized plastic work boxes. Making things easier to find will save you valuable time and make your workspace a more efficient one.

Organizing your paperwork is just another aspect of having an efficient work place. Make sure your patterns are easy to find. You could try labeling each piece or even having a different color for each pattern if you use colored cards for them. The patterns can be filed according to size, date of creation or family tree. Keep a note of the last number of each pattern that you have made, particularly if it is a limited edition. Even if it is an open edition, many bear artists still number each bear.

If you produce limited editions for various shops and galleries, keep a book or card system on your editions. Include all the details such as date, pattern, size, mohair, edition size, special characteristics, who it was for, and whether it was sold or on consignment.

Keep a book for the names and addresses of all the people who requested a catalogue from you, and mark against their name if they subsequently ordered a bear. This will give you a good idea of the response you are getting from your catalogue and you will be able to work out the costs and returns of printing, mailing and sales. This list is your collector base and can be a valuable mailing list for your promotional material. Some bear artists even send out regular newsletters to their collectors. A visitor's book, used if people visit your studio or at shows, is a good way of adding to your collector base.

Make sure that your stationery, business cards and catalogues do not run out before you reorder them, particularly if you have a show coming up where you will need them. Keep a correspondence file and answer all your mail.

Bookkeeping is also an essential part of every business, no matter how small. Find a good accountant to guide you, have a separate business account and maintain your records. A petty cash book, vehicle log, and stamp book can also help you and your accountant. Find out from your accountant what your claimable expenses are and keep records and receipts of these for tax time. Having a professional approach in this area will make your record keeping easier. It also helps prove your status as a professional in your chosen career and therefore you will be able to claim certain tax deductions.

Business Etiquitte

There is certain etiquette that should be followed in this business as in others, but unfortunately not everyone knows the rules. Etiquette in this instance is simply good behavior or common sense. All you need to do is to think about your actions and their consequences.

If you sell to a shop, out of respect to that store's owner do not put your full address and telephone number on the swing tag. If you do you might be promoting yourself but you may also be stopping a sale for the shop. The shop is already promoting you by stocking your work and it is not fair for the shop if their customer sees your tag and approaches you directly rather than buying that bear. If you do supply a fully detailed swing tag, don't be surprised or annoyed if you discover it has been removed before the bear reaches the store's shelves. It is quite all right to put your name and logo on your swing tag, but just be more general in terms of your place of origin,
for example, "Wisconsin, USA" or "Sydney, Australia".

If you wholesale as well as retail, the shops' retail price may be higher than yours, depending on their markup. They have significant overhead such as rent for their premises which you do not have if you work from home, and they are entitled to charge what they like as long as they agree not to sell below your cost price. In order not to be seen as undercutting the stores you supply to, why not agree to supply exclusive one-of-a-kind or limited edition bears? That way the store will have something that no other retailer will have (including you) and they are justified in charging a little more for their special stock.

It is a good idea to try and avoid shows near retailers whom you supply to, so that there is no potential conflict between you and your store. If it is unavoidable that there is a show near a retailer that you wholesale to, it is polite to let them know that you will be there. Reassure them that you will not have identical stock, and should the store also be taking trading space at the same show suggest they might choose not to put your stock on their table.

Do not stock stores that are too near each other or you may well flood your own market and make your retailers unhappy. Both the collectors and the retailer likes to think they are getting something special.

If you have produced a limited edition for a store, do not continue to use that bear in your normal range. Even the name of the bear can cause problems if it continues to be used after you had promised and delivered a store exclusive.

Work with the retailer on your exclusives. They may well have their own ideas of what they want from you and they know their customer base better than you. Send a prototype or number one of the edition for approval before working on the rest of the edition. The retailer may be keen to emphasize a certain characteristic of your work when they promote you, so they may well want your work to reflect that. (For example, the bears wearing hats with handmade silk roses, or the bears' paws embroidered, or the bears' noses made of molded leather.)

Should you use someone else's design, make sure you ask their permission to do so, especially if it is to be sold as you may be contravening the copyright. As a courtesy you should always credit the designer on your swing tag.

Answer all your mail even if you are not able to supply the bears requested. If you have a computer it may save you a lot of time to have several form letters on file where you can just insert the date and the relevant name. One for "thank you, but I do not do wholesale at the present time", one for "thank you for your inquiry, but I do not sell my patterns", one for "thank you for the show invitation but I am fully booked, maybe next year" and so on can be very handy to have!

Staying Healthy

In order to last in any career it is necessary to look after yourself mentally as well as physically, and this is especially important when you are running your own business, and when that business involves your own physical labor. If you are a sole trader, that is working alone in your business, any down time you might have means a time of no income so staying healthy should always be a high priority.

As bear making is very labor intensive, particularly if you are a hand sewer, there is always a risk of some form of RSI (repetitive strain injury). For hand sewers the most vulnerable body part seems to be the joint at the base of the thumbs and the thumb joints, for machine sewers it is often the elbows. Inflammation and stiffness of the joints can indicate the onset of arthritic conditions, so take care to exercise and loosen your hands and arms, and try not to do the same thing day after day. Break down your work schedule into perhaps sewing one day, stuffing another and paperwork on another day. Overworking the same joint with the same activity day after day, for example the elbow joint when stuffing, can really put a strain on it.

As well as varying your routine, try to vary the tools you use. It is very easy to get into a habit of using the same tools and holding them in the same way, but those tools may not be ergonomically correct for the human hand. A good example is using a stick or chopstick to stuff with, where you are using a lot of force with an angled wrist. This puts excess pressure on the inside edge of your wrist joint (nearest your thumb) and can lead to strain, ganglions and carpal tunnel syndrome.

Rotate the use of your straight stuffing sticks with the T-shaped stuffing sticks, where you hold the horizontal handle in your palm with the shaft of the stick between your second and third finger and form a fist to push with. This keeps your wrist straight and much stronger.

Find more ergonomic tools like this to help make your work easier and extend your working life. The new spring-loaded scissors without thumb grips, such as the Fiskars brand, are great for taking the pressure off your thumb joints when you have a lot of cutting out to do.

As well as finding safe tools, keep your tools safe. The points of needle-nosed pliers can be covered by slipping on a cut length from a plastic drinking straw. Long doll needles are best kept in a case or stuck in a wine cork so you do not find them accidentally whilst rummaging through your tool box!

Be careful when using your tools too. Long doll needles in particular can be lethal. Always pull away from yourself when pulling eye threads through the head. Needles have been known to go right into chests to the sternum bone, and right through noses, forearms or hands! Also never leave needles or pins stuck into the upholstered arms of your chair or the cushion on your chair. You can easily forget they are there - until you sit on them or rest your arm on them. Always keep track of all your needles and pins, if one drops to the floor pick it up straight away or the dog, cat or child might find it before you do. Try and save yourself any expensive veterinary or pediatrics bills involving your pins and needles!

Thimbles in metal and leather, and leather finger stalls and sleeves can help protect your fingers. There are also special fingerless gloves for sewers that can help ease stiff hands and improve circulation.

Take care of your spine by making sure you have a good seat to work in and that you do not slump to a more comfortable position. If your back is not kept straight you may find that you will end up putting extra pressure on your neck and upper back as your head slumps forward and your shoulders round. Make sure that your favorite chair is giving you adequate support. If necessary use one of those small lumbar support cushions to keep the base of your spine pushed forward.

Keep yourself fit generally and you will lead a longer, healthier life. Having regular breaks and going for walks will not only be good for your dog if you have one, it will be good for your back and your heart. Bear making is a very sedentary job and it is depressingly easy to lose fitness and gain weight when you spend your life sitting down. Getting out and about helps to clear the cobwebs out of your head too. Some very important bear making ideas can emerge while walking in the park with the dog!

Look after your eyes. Regular breaks are good for the eyes, too, as bear making can be a real strain on them. Make sure you work with a good light, and make any important decisions regarding color matching during daylight hours rather than at night.

Remember to protect your lungs too. Wear a dust mask when stuffing bears or even when cutting them out if the mohair irritates you. Long term effects of flying fur and stuffing on bear makers have not been clinically tested, but at the very least you could end up with a nasty fur ball! In rare instances, long term use of mohair has been known to cause irritation and allergies.

Don't take on too much or you may find that your bear making career will become as stressful as the one you left, and you left it for that very reason! Have aspirations and aims but don't promise more than you can deliver. Keep the joy of making bears an important part of your business. If you find you are getting bogged down in making that shop's order of a limited edition of 25 bears, take some time out to do something that you want. It may just be half a day for designing a new bear that you have been thinking about, but having that new pattern just itching to be made will give you something to look forward to after the hard slog of the order is over.

Working for a show can be a treat rather than a deadline if you approach it the right way. Plan your time. Don't leave things until they become a last minute panic. Use time to be creative. You might have to produce limited editions for wholesale clients, but why not use shows to produce all new prototypes or those ideas for one-of-a-kinds that you have been thinking about.

If you do get to the stage where you are feeling worn out by it all, then take some time off to refresh yourself. Don't push yourself too hard and make bears when you really do not want to or are not well enough to, as your feelings can be reflected in the quality of your workmanship. Looking after yourself will not only ensure that you are healthy but will also infuse your creations with happiness and serenity, and who wouldn't want to buy a piece of that?

The Path to Success

All the tips given in this book will hopefully make sense, and some may help make your path to success a little easier. Success is a very personal thing and it depends on your aims and ambitions. Many people do not want to be the best in the world at something but are happy with the personal satisfaction that their creations bring. There are some wonderful artists who are never heard of and never sell their work because they are perfectly happy creating their art for themselves. There are some for whom public recognition is important, while others would like the fortune without the fame. Whatever you want out of your chosen career it is important to aim for goals, even if your only aim is to continue doing what you love doing.

The reason that most of us started making bears as a business was because we discovered that we loved the creative process, the satisfaction it gave us and the joy it gave the recipients of the bears. It is important not to lose sight of that. If we do, we lose the momentum for continuing with bear making as a profession. Don't burn out by taking on too much, too fast. Pace yourself and love what you do because you are doing what you love.

Suppliers Index

All these bear making supply companies will provide comprehensive mail order catalogues on request. Fabric sample swatches are also available.

USA:

Edinburgh Imports, Inc.
P.O. Box 340
Newbury Park, CA 91319-0340
Ph. (805) 376-1700
Fax (805) 376-1711

Intercal Trading Group
1760 Monrovia
Suite A-17
Costa Mesa, CA 92627
Ph. (714) 645-9396
Fax (715) 645-5471

Australia:

Beary Cheap Bear Supplies
P.O. Box 2465 Burleigh MDC QLD. 4220
Fax 0050-833393

Dee Glossop Teddy Bears and Accessories
86 Model Farms Rd.
NSW 2153.
Ph. & Fax (02) 9686-1682.

Gerry's Teddies & Craft Designs
30 Upper John Street
Rosewod, QLD 4340
Ph. & Fax (075) 641-479

UK:

Oakley Fabrics Ltd.
Dept. HG
8 May St.
Luton LU1 3QY
Ph. (01582) 424-828 or 34733
Fax (01582) 445-274

Bibliography

Brewer, Kim & Rössel-Waugh, Carol-Lynn. *The Official Price Guide to Antique and Modern Teddy Bears.*
    House of Collectibles, NY 1990.
Ceislik, Jürgen and Marianne. *Button in Ear - The History of The Teddy Bear and His Friends.*
    Marianne Ceislik Verlag, 1989.
Cockrill, Pauline. *The Teddy Bear Encyclopedia.* Dorling Kindersley Ltd. UK 1993.
Mullins, Linda. *Teddy Bears Past and Present -- A Collector's Identification Guide.* Hobby House Press, Inc., 1986.
Yelland, Jill. *The Art of Minding Your Own Business.* Press For Success, Aust. 1994.